"Dr. Will Taegel carries the gift of story-telling. His Native American roots provide a deep wisdom that comes through the gifts of deep reflection and connection to Nature, the Spirit World, and the power of the spoken word to teach through a story and in writing."

— Angeles Arrien,
Cultural Anthropologist

"I just read WILD HEART and found it fascinating. Dr. Taegel is onto a major piece of writing. I love the notion of a nature deficit disorder as the condition of our culture. I am taken with how all sacred inner councils must make room for the shadow. I look forward to reading other books in the series."

— Jim Garrison,
President of Wisdom University

"Dr. Taegel's words may well help readers recall their natural affinity with the Infinite. He attests that there is a realm beyond the usual that he and his Earthtribe folk have seen in their visions and concludes that we are all called to this realm from beyond ourselves. To respond to this call is the most important move human beings can make."

— Huston Smith,
author of *The World's Religions*
Subject of Bill Moyer's PBS Special

Dr. Taegel honors the complexity of the spiral journey in what we would call a "psycho-spiritual process", a process that includes both the psychological work and the spiritual work necessary to move among differing levels of reality that can eventually lead us to our essence."

— Hal and Sidra Stone,
creators of Voice Dialogue

THE SACRED COUNCIL
Of Your

WILD HEART

NATURE'S HOPE IN EARTH'S CRISIS

The Sacred Mentor Series

Dr. Will Taegel

2nd Tier Publishing

Published by:
  2nd Tier Publishing
  501 Wimberley Oaks
  Wimberley, TX 78676, U.S.A.

ISBN 978-0-578-05832-0

Cover design and photograph by Dan Gauthier
Book design by Dan Gauthier

Contents

Part III Sacred Councils Bond

Part IV The Web of Sacred Councils: Wild Heart Stories of Hope In Crisis

About the Author

Texas native Will Taegel grew up on the Llano Estacado where he began his lifelong and intimate relationship with Nature. Choosing an integrative approach early on, Dr. Taegel received his Masters at Emory University and his Doctorate at the University of California, Berkeley, SFTS, all the while being inspired to explore his Native American heritage and being traditionally trained in the ways of the Shaman. Always fascinated and happily challenged by human psychology and one's relationships to the self and others, Dr. Taegel conducted a successful psychotherapy practice for 35 years which evolved into his current role of a sought-after Mentor. Dr. Taegel has written 8 books weaving together nature, spirituality, psychology and relationship and has recently been appointed Dean of the Faculty, Wisdom University. He and his spouse, Judith Yost, founded a three decades old spiritual community called The Earthtribe.

Introduction to the Book Series: The Sacred Mentor

Do you have a crucial role in the future of our planet?

My proposal in this book series advances the notion that the Evolutionary Spirit seeks to move through humans to mentor Earth's process. At crucial times, when life conditions call forth staggering challenges and new possibilities, certain humans make themselves available and thus mentor the spiral of unfolding awareness and compassion. They tune into larger energy fields (internet and beyond), and information passes through to them. They become Leaders of the Spiral of Evolution, and frequently they form Sacred Councils as a matrix for evolutionary leaps.

We know through the newer sciences the universe is expanding into ever more complex patterns. The question arises: Where is it going?

Scientist Brian Swimme addresses that question: "The Universe is evolving toward a point of every aspect of the universe knowing every other aspect in its fullness."[1] Put another way, the Universe evolves in waves of greater and greater complexity and waves of human awareness broad enough to address the complexity. This flavor of awareness makes possible, even probable, a more mature intimacy. How does this information involve you, the reader? I will speak more to this issue in the last chapter of the first book, *WILD HEART*.

Sacred Mentors are humans and living systems awakening to the larger story. To enlarge the Universe Story we will need to:

- Become *The Sacred Council*, by learning to access your *Wild Heart*, Book 1
- Unfold through *The Sacred Spiral*, Book 2
- Journey through *The Sacred Quest*, Book 3
- View through *The Sacred Lens*, Book 4
- Develop through *The Sacred Ceremony*, Book 5

Prologue:
The Sacred Council of
Your Wild Heart

In my career as a psychotherapist, I voyaged through two major whitewater narrows, tumbling about as I hit rock bottom. The first major turbulence arose when my clients obtained relief from their presenting symptoms and asked me to guide them to a larger vision of the world.

They asked deeper questions beyond conventional psychological models, questions about the ultimate meaning of life. I didn't have a larger vision myself, so that presented a problem. My childhood spiritual maps had been cast aside, along with the immediate relevance of my graduate work in theology, to tackle the gritty issues of everyday life. Neither map was sufficient for the questions arising out of the crises of my adult world—divorce, death of my father, and financial stress. A few hints of larger cosmic maps were emerging, but I wasn't sure enough to share them publicly.

A second and related passage through white water came after practicing for two decades. At last, I developed a spiritual practice relevant to my life. It was the 1980's, and Nature-based spirituality emerged as a personal pathway, yet my efforts were quite tentative. I had not extended my personal, spiritual practices into the treatment process with my psychotherapy clients for a number of reasons. Chief among these reluctances was the pressure of the psychological profession to conform to the usual standards of professional and clinical practice. Serving on the Texas State Board of Examiners of Social Psychotherapists for seven years, and, as Chairperson for two years, I had assisted in shaping these standards of practice.

As a profession we were sensitive at the time to our place in the larger society. Psychotherapy had finally entered the mainstream, but deep suspicions remained with the population-at-large. Let me give you an example. As Chairperson of the State Board of Examiners, I was called on to testify before the Senate of the State of Texas. The Senators were reviewing the various licensing boards to see if they would renew the license for another four years. Those politically opposed to this psychotherapy license had lined up a Senator from East Texas as their champion. He had blood in his eyes and our profession in the cross hairs of his big political guns.

At the hearings I spoke as Chairperson for some time about the technical definitions of our profession in support of the continuation of the license. When I paused to catch my breath in this raucous political setting, he interrupted me.

"Dr. Taegel, I am from East Texas, and I don't understand these high fallutin' concepts," he spoke not so much to me but to the packed galleries. "Is psychotherapy (he dragged out that word with a deep Southern drawl) something like palm reading? We have such a person on the side of the road near my hometown. Do you license such persons?"

I don't recall my response; caught off guard, I mainly stumbled.

No wonder I was reluctant to color outside the lines with that kind of political oversight; yet, I knew in my heart of hearts my clients and students would benefit from the Nature-based growth experiences that Judith Yost, my spouse, and I had created. Some of our clients attended these wilderness experiences, but I, and other therapists in the group, were uneasy. What would the State Board of Examiners say if something went wrong? I kept picturing myself having to answer to people such as the Senator I just described. I had a powerful inner tension between my standards of practice and the urge to journey into the eco-spiritual domains calling to me.

With this description as a cultural context, we can move to a specific situation. A client—I will call her Marjo—came into my office with an ongoing depression. We had been working together for over a year. My office was large, measuring about 15' by 20'. In one corner, we had an assortment of expressive tools—art supplies, sand trays, and encounter batons for anger training. We were not bolted to our chairs the way many therapists worked at the time, so it wasn't movement we were missing. Nevertheless, something was missing. We sat there. I could see in Marjo's body posture we were stuck.

> Eco-spiritual means an approach to a person's spiritual path which begins with a deep connection to the ecology such as being moved by the majesty of the Grand Canyon. The power of the ecology awakens the inner spirit. This approach is in contrast to a spirituality that begins with stimulation from the written or spoken word or subjective inquiry.

An intuition floated to the surface of my interior like bubbles in a pond. In a burst of enthusiasm, I suggested we don our coats and go for a walk. Marjo blinked. Such a proposal was beyond the norm. Beset with chronic depression, she had seen a number of psychotherapists and psychiatrists through the years. She knew this walking option was different because she had tried nearly everything, including medication. They had not helped, and she wanted relief. After all, what could a few strides into the outdoors hurt?

Standards of practice notwithstanding, why was a walk such a big deal in which I took the arm of a client to cross a busy street? For me, at the time, it was. Perhaps, it was the thought of a state regulation instructing psychotherapists not to touch their clients for any reason. The regulation was set forth to protect clients from sexual abuse by a person in power, and with good reason. Yet, slavish adherence to the rules tended to squeeze the life out of my work. Did being a professional mean giving up the common human decency of a helping hand or a pat on the back? With these thoughts in the back of my mind, we left the office.

Once outside, we walked through parking lots and across busy streets. Marjo talked. We walked. At first, I noticed nothing different. Depressive conversation is characterized by pessimism, hopelessness, and, often, victim mentality. That talk continued until we came to an urban pocket park. A giant oak tree thrust itself into view to our right as we ambled down a shady sidewalk. One of its limbs extended out from the trunk, curved downward, and touched the ground some fifteen feet in the distance. The curved limb formed a nice place to sit, and sit, we did.

Marjo's eyes lit up. She talked of trees from childhood and a creek behind her home-of-origin where she played. When we left the tree, there was a change in energy. We walked, and she said, "I don't feel so depressed. How strange!"

When we returned to the office, we both noticed a huge difference when we stepped into air-conditioned space. Compared to the out-of-doors the room was slightly stale, not as alive. The contrast was palpable. Something remarkable—even extraordinary—had happened on the walk. She had hope written across her face. She and I had acquired something, some energy, an untamed force we couldn't quite name on the walk. Her Wild Heart had not entered her consciousness, but it was knocking on the door.

At that moment I recalled an experience I had with Bear Heart, my long-time shamanic teacher. He had come from New Mexico to visit me in Houston where I was in practice. We spent a whole day driving and walking around the city talking, but he seemed to be aiming at something he hadn't spoken. After a few hours, I asked him what we were doing. He replied, "We are searching for the Wild Heart of the city. Every city, no matter how urban, has a specific place still beating with the untamed Spirit reaching out to awaken humans."

Toward the end of the day, we came to a park and Bear Heart spoke again, "This is it. The city organizes itself around this particular spot." I nodded, but at that time I really couldn't feel the energy he described. The subtlety was beyond my perceptive abilities. I now noticed the oak tree so crucial to Marjo on our walk was the very one Bear Heart had leaned against. An inner resource long forgotten lurched into my memory, and I suspected something similar had transpired for Marjo.

Perhaps this all sounds too far-fetched—a trifle melodramatic or excessively idealistic. How could a simple walk in a city park offer so much? Is there room for a skeptical voice in our conversation?

About that time Judith and I were invited by the American Academy of Psychotherapists to give a workshop for therapists at their annual conference. It was held that year at Newport Beach, California, in a five star conference facility. We summoned our courage and offered a workshop titled

> This book addresses what happened, the hope Marjo and I found, and the beginnings of a map that assisted in our navigating her crisis.

Eco-Spiritual Therapy. Fifteen brave souls signed up, including several leading psychotherapists from across the nation. We were nervous. In the men's room at the wash basin, Bob, a psychiatrist I knew casually, pounded the cabinet like a drum to announce in sarcasm to all present Will's new therapy. "The natives are restless," he laughed. His humor only amplified my nerves.

Next to the conference hotel there was, as you might guess, a golf course. Golf courses receive poor press in environmental circles, but they do provide green space in crowded urban areas. We hatched the notion to take the group outside—a radical idea at the time—and to sit on the edge of the golf course.

We dodged a few golf balls and proceeded with our plan. In a moment of further spontaneity, we suggested the participants take off their shoes and feel the grass on the bottom of their feet. By that time in our continued experiments, we recognized the importance of such connections with Nature. Even if the client was conscious for a passing moment, something was awakened that was crucial to the therapeutic process.

Off to my right in the circle, I noticed a prominent psychoanalyst from New York City, about sixty years of age. I'll call her Dr. Joan. I wondered how she might respond to such an experimental assignment. At first, Dr. Joan grumbled something about *kid stuff* and muttered under her breath about the whole endeavor being *unprofessional and back to nature crap.* I watched her closely because

I sensed potential trouble. Her face clouded. Tears rolled. Judith and I intuitively moved over to sit cross-legged in front of her. She continued to sob. At last she caught her breath in what seemed like an hour but had actually been a minute or so.

"That's the first time I felt grass on my feet since I was a child." She now had a softness in her face and a depth of strength arising through an expanding chest and a straightening of her spine.

She told her story of growing up in New York City where she visited Central Park with her father. Together, they had walked barefoot on summer mornings, feeling fresh dew on their feet. Over fifty years had passed since she allowed such an experience in her life. It was, she explained, too messy. What had once been lost to her was now returning. But what? Was this the Wild Heart of Nature expanding her chest, lifting her spine, and looking out at me through glistening eyes?

> *"I believe a leaf of grass is no less than the journey work of the stars."*
> Ralph Waldo Emerson, *Leaves of Grass*

We corresponded for awhile, did the psychoanalyst, Dr. Joan, and I; she marveled at how that moment had brought forth a hidden participant in her inner world—the natural, even magical, little girl. Puzzled, I talked about Dr. Joan's experience with Native Americans, tribal elders who were training me in the ways of the Indigenous mind, and they told me Dr. Joan had experienced soul retrieval. That was news to me at that stage of my development since that phrase was a distant boyhood memory, covered over by years of traditional graduate education.

This book attends to soul retrieval as I have come to understand it. We will journey together into our personal and planetary crises. I will propose that our hope for moving through planetary and personal traumas resides in a return to our awareness zone of the Nature-based self, that dormant side of ourselves just waiting to council us as we connect with sitting in oak trees in urban parks and touching our feet to grass at the edge of golf courses.

In experiences like the ones mentioned, I was reshaping my definition of *wilderness*. Could *wilderness* refer to a dimension much larger than a place in Alaska or Yellowstone National Park? Is there a self implicit in Nature nearby, an Indigenous self, seeking entrance into our awareness as with Dr. Joan? If so, what is the role of this Wild Heart in shaping our future?

Part I of this book aims at what I see as the call of Grandmother Nature through the pressure of our current, worldwide environmental crisis. She implores us to be aware, active participants in the shaping of a new direction for Earth. It is Her Wild Heart seeking to renew us. Having stated that theme, questions arise. Am I advocating a simple return to the noble savage in the manner of philosopher Jean-Jacque Rousseau in his *Discourse*? Am I joining the romanticism of the 18th Century in its revolt against the rational in favor of emotion and intuition?

> A *wilderness*, home of our Wild Heart within, is any condition in Nature that challenges our usual control. Just *eight paces* from my office door I start a walk in the rain with a student as the wind turns our umbrellas inside out. In those eight paces I move from culture to wilderness, home of our Wild Heart. The variable conditions let me know how little control I have. Wild weather opens me to the possibility within.

Part II offers a map of our interior world, one I call *The Sacred Council*. This section explores an approach that transcends the romanticism of the noble savage but includes its truth. We will encounter the necessary inclusion of the wild-hearted self in our council, a crucial component if we are to move through the Earth's transition now in motion like a runaway train. The Wild Heart, while absolutely necessary, is invited to sit in the council, not dominate it. The Sacred Council is presided over by a presence called *the aware ego*. How that works will be addressed in Part II.

Part III offers a preliminary map of how our inner world relates to the external world. First, we will explore our tendency to conflict with others. Then, we will see how our so-called positive bonding patterns with life around us may not be sufficient. Finally, we will enter the powerful domain and experience of intimacy, natural intimacy, as exactly the resource we need to navigate the white waters of overwhelming conditions arising in our personal lives and magnified on the world stage.

Part IV offers shamanic stories as humans rediscover hope and encouragement in the current crisis through their deep relationships with non-human energy forms—birds, trees, canyons, mountains, and quantum waves. These stories also call forth the Wild Heart—the sublimity of untamed Nature—to sit in the council.

> *"When the Earth is sick, the animals will begin to disappear. When that happens, the Warriors of the Rainbow will come to save them.*
>
> Chief Si'ahl, 1864

> *"We do not inherit the Earth from our Ancestors, we borrow it from our children."*
>
> Bear Heart, mentoring the author, 1982

In this discussion, dear reader, I invite you to open yourself to a possibility—the potential we all have to take even a short walk into the Wild Heart to find Nature's Hope In Earth's Crisis. Your wild potential may be only eight paces, or less, from where you sit. The Grand Attractor, a mysterious and impossible to define Force, pulls you out of the confines of your culture into the hands of the Divine Wild Heart. It is the same Impulse beating behind the Big Bang. It is the same wildness pushing the edges of the Universe. Once you clasp this forceful hand and continue to hold on for dear life, you can be led to your true nature within Nature.

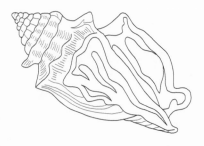

PART I

The Call of the Era of Crisis

"Only with the moment of time represented by the present century has one species—man—acquired significant power to alter the nature of his world."
— Rachel Carson
ecologist and biologist

"Evidence is mounting from many di⬚erent scientific disciplines that the Earth's natural systems are already undergoing rapid change. We need to act now to reduce heat-trapping gas emission for the sake of our children and the other species with whom we share the planet."
— Pamela Mason
Dean of Earth Sciences,
Stanford University

"Our nation has both an obligation and self-interest in facing head-on the serious environmental, economic and national security threat posed by global warming."
— John McCain
   conservative politician

"This is precisely why the current situation concerning global warming is so worrying. All the measurement and reports of dire consequences still do not accurately forecast with any precision the rate of deterioration."
— Richard David Hames
   The Five Literacies of Global Leadership,
   p. 81

1

Sounding the Conch

"Tell me a story about the conch shell, Pa Pa," Katie, my six year old granddaughter, looked at me with inquiring eyes and made this request. She held the tribal conch and rubbed the oil of her hands into its already shiny surface with tender caresses. The sight of her holding the conch next to her heart took me back many decades to similar experiences in my childhood and questions I once had.

The story of the conch Katie held tenderly tumbled out as I stitched together various accounts filtering through my memory faintly informed by historical events and family stories.

The magnificent conch shell descended to the lowly job of door stop in the West Texas home of my boyhood days. Its primary job consisted of keeping an interior French door from banging against the living room wall. The High Plains winds blew through the open windows in a house with no air conditioning and offered a significant challenge to restraining the door from swinging into its own destruction. On the other hand the wind would occasionally be strong enough to move through the opening in the conch and emit faint whispers, gentle allurements calling to and firing my imagination.

"Are you sure the wind blew that hard, Pa Pa?" Katie challenged elder exaggeration.

"It still blows like that in West Texas. Sometimes the dust even penetrates the cracks of the vaults at the local bank," I spoke convincingly. She still looked skeptical but interested in the story line.

One warm June day when I had nothing to do, I picked up the conch and walked with bare feet across hardwood floors outside to the front yard. There I sat in a cave hollowed out of thick branches underneath a spreading juniper bush. The image of someone blowing the shell danced across my eyes and echoed in my ears. I put it to my lips and blew as forcefully as I could, imitating the vision in my mind. Slowly, a deep resonance emerged from the innards of the spiral shell. The power of the low-pitched vibration moved through me in a profound manner difficult to put into words.

All afternoon the calls of the conch wafted out of the juniper cave until my mother came out on the front porch to see what all the racket was. She answered the very question you asked me about the conch, Katie.

"What did she say, Pa Pa?" Katie's question box was filled to the brim.

She told me about my great grand mother, Louiza, who came to Texas one summer in the 1840's. Louiza was born in a Shawnee Village a decade earlier. Later, I would hear another part of the story from a relative who recounted a harrowing tale of Louiza's mother,Tilitha. It seems Texas Slave traders dragged her out of her Shawnee village along with Louiza, and that's how our family ended up in Texas. Louiza, herself a half breed, married a slave trader from Kentucky.

"What happened then?" Katie's eyes glowed with interest.

Widowed on a ranch in Central Texas in pre-Civil War days, Louiza was visited by Tonkawas who were on a hunting trip a distance from their home grounds on the Gulf Coast. The Tonkawas brought a gift with them from the Gulf beaches—the ceremonial conch shell you hold in your hands. Already old the conch shell had felt many mouths of native elders blow through its opening in important Native ceremonies. According to the story the Tonakwas presented their deeply treasured conch shell, the source of generations of healing in their tribe, to Louiza.

"Why? Pa Pa," Katie wrinkled her brow.

Louiza must have been quite a sight in the Texas rolling hills. She was a woman running a ranch when women didn't have the right to own property. She must have been known far and wide as a Shawnee, a Native, who owned property when local Commanches still lived a nomadic life style, bedeviling the area ranchers. I can imagine the shell passing from the Tonkawas hands to Louiza's out of deep respect, even awe at her accomplishments. Katie, I am just filling in the blanks here in a family story. Family stories are sometimes factual, sometimes not.

Louiza kept the conch in a prized place in the ranch house. Each day she blew it to greet the morning and then later to call her twin sons in from the field where they worked. During those very precarious times, she blew the shell to warn her sons and the hired hands of an imminent danger. Violent prejudice directed toward Native Americans, and women for that matter, was rampant. Their very survival depended on their hearing the sound of the conch.

Intuitively, she knew the sound of the conch tuned her into the larger resources of the Universe to survive in an extremely challenging situation. Many years later her son, Lee, your great, great grand father, strapped the shell to the saddle of his horse as he road for two hard weeks North and West to the Texas Panhandle where I grew up.

"How did you get the conch, Pa Pa?" Katie toyed with the relic in her hands respectfully.

From the day my mother told me her version of the story and heard the sounds coming from the juniper cave, she said I was to have it. Later, as I began my training with Native elders, she gifted me with the conch. Although she hadn't kept up the ancient traditions and was unaware of many parts of the story, she sensed something special about the conch. So for six decades I have used its vibrations as a link to the Sacred in prayers and meditations.

Scientists track the evolution of music in the spiral of the human story. Modern humans appeared some 200,000 years ago. It took them 150,000 years with the same triune brain we have to develop the hand ax. Think of that for a moment. Our species required ¾ of the time we have been on the planet to evolve the lowly hand ax. Astonishingly: that was it! Still the invention of this tool constituted a major leap in the human endeavor. We are indebted to the sacred leadership that gave us this tool through an expansion of consciousness. Out of expanded consciousness emerged this crucial invention.

In this book series we will track the story of human consciousness in community and probe a number of key puzzles, including why it took so long to invent that tool. The short answer here is that humans were too busy surviving even to use music to express themselves. The powers of the human neo-cortex focused entirely on food and shelter. Only when they became skilled enough at survival to have leisure time were they able to tune into the larger resources of the universe.

> **Calling the Sacred Council:** The presence of artifacts in early burials without any apparent practical function is interpreted by scientists as an expression of symbolic behavior. Thus, conchs constitute one of the earliest indications of human consciousness to expand beyond practical survival into metaphoric and symbolic meaning. Humans blowing the conch present us with a first in symbolic leadership, a key to sacred meaning. The conch became the primary tool for calling humans into Sacred Council.

At the 36,800 year mark of the evolutionary spiral the first human stopped to take a breath from the rigors of survival and to express herself in music. An unusual sensation must have welled up from the depths, an urge to make music, to feel the vibrations, and to send them forth. That must have been quite a moment, one of the crucial pivots in the spiral of consciousness.

What was the first instrument? A hollow branch? A reed from the bank of a river? Two rocks struck together? A bone flute? Beating on a hollow log? Archeology points toward the earliest undisputed musical instrument as conch shells found in European caves, so asserts a massive National Geographic Study.[1]

Picture in your mind's eye a young woman, such as my grand daughter, Katie, hoisting a conch shell from a beach. The top of its spiral shell knocked off or opened in some unknown manner. No other person had ever thought to put lips to the opening and blow. Following an intuitive impulse outside the pattern of her archaic culture, she blows just as I did in the juniper cave.

The trajectory of the spiral of human consciousness turns with this first sound, the sound of the first music, the initial human music in the Universe, at least within the realm of our knowledge. It floated forth with those maiden notes to join with what the ancients called the music of the spheres.

Sacred Council means bringing into the aware zone the inner and outer aspects of the Universe crucial to this moment in the human story.

Just as the ceremonial conch called to my fore parents in the fields of the Texas Hill Country, warning them of danger, warming their hearts, mentoring them in awareness, and pulling them to the next level of evolutionary leadership, so the conch calls us during this crucial time.

What is the tone of the call?

> *"You are brilliant, and the Earth is hiring."*
>
> Paul Hawken,
> Sustainable Entrepreneur

2

Leaning into the Questions

For years my mother, Juanita, and I wrote a column for a local newspaper where she lived in West Texas. In exploring possible themes we chewed on a conversation she had with her father, Lee, about our family land. He was a key founder of the town in the late 1800's. He worked hard and obtained several thousand acres. Underneath this rich land lay one of the great aquifers of the Earth, the Ogallala.

Though the land was rich, the weather was unpredictable and punctuated with intense droughts. Lee punched a hole in the ground and discovered the pure and tasty water of the Ogallala and appreciated the gift of sustenance for his family. The windmills he and his contemporaries built to pull drinking water for themselves and their milk cows became an archetypal symbol for the area. Some years the weather danced with the land to produce bountiful crops. Other growing seasons parched the crops with lack of rain, leaving farming and ranching families in severe distress.

The dust bowl of the 1930's arrived hand in hand with The Great Depression. Humans searched desperately for solutions. Lee's contemporaries discovered irrigation, using the combustion engine to pull the water out of the depths of the aquifer. For many, it seemed a jackpot solution at the time. Although Lee had lost a fortune in the depression through bank failures and needed the extra income, he harbored profound questions about irrigation and the taking of the ground water. He stumped around the Panhandle speaking out forcefully against the plan to use the aquifer for irrigation. Something about treating the Earth in this fashion did not sit right with him.

Incredible pressure mounted for Lee to draw on the underground water for his benefit. He was a community leader, but he chose not to throw the weight of his leadership in the direction of water for profit. As long as he was alive, he did not allow the mining of water on his land other than for drinking. Lee saw his leadership as a sacred trust, and that included conserving the water.

In 1985 I sat in the office of J.B. Wheeler, President of a bank in the Panhandle town of Plainview, talking about my grandfather as part of an interview for a column in the local newspaper. Lee died about the time I was born, but I have always felt close to him. J.B. spoke fondly of how Lee mentored him, offering wise council about land and water. Mr. Wheeler deeply respected my grandfather, even considered him a mentor, but he disagreed with Lee's position on water. His bank was built on the wealth provided by the water pulled from the ground. He listened to Lee's counsel on many subjects, but not water.

Soon after Lee's death, my father, W.R. Taegel, and his generation of farmer/ranchers drilled thousands of holes into the aquifer, perhaps smiling smugly at Lee's traditional ways. The new technology of irrigation was spectacularly successful. The land sprouted with green crops: wheat, cotton, corn, and soybeans. These were my childhood years during World War II. I hiked in the beautiful canyons near our land oblivious to the water controversy. The springs, overflow of the Ogallala, poured forth out of the canyon walls, providing me with a swimming hole for delightful boyhood refreshment. I assumed it would always be so.

The springs and canyon ecology were my Sacred Council in childhood. I turned to junipers, eagles, sandhill cranes, quail, big sky, powerful wind, and open spaces for my spiritual guidance.

Many wonderful people entered my life, but they were secondary in importance to wild creatures in feeding my soul, my essence.

One day I went to my favorite swimming hole in a canyon, and was stunned to see there was no water. I was ten years old, and it was 1950. In one short decade the adults of my world had used so much water the aquifer level lowered to the point the springs ran no more. I was the last of my kind to swim in the sacred water so treasured by indigenous people around the world.

A profound sadness moved through me as I looked at the drying moss and the now stagnant pool. A crucial aspect of my Sacred Council had died, though I could not put it into words at the time. I could not know rationally the far-reaching effect on the environment the depletion of the water resources would have on the environment. I could not know water would someday become gold. I could not know the next century would see the waters of the world threatened

"Water has become a highly precious resource. There are some places where a barrel of water costs more than a barrel of oil."

Lloyd Axworthy,
Foreign Minister of Canada

by a profligate life style benefiting my family. I could not know some people in my neighborhood would pay $400 a month for their water utilities by 2010.

I did know tears rolled down my cheeks, salty in my mouth.

Would the disappearance of this wonder of natural springs wake up the users? The decision-makers in my hometown, with their limited vision, adopted a mantra of no harm, no foul, no problem. The farmers—the adults of my world—drilled deeper and deeper, until they reached red bed, an indication of the bottom of what seemed to be an unlimited supply of water. This point in the story draws us near to the question I asked my mother as we wrestled with a theme for our weekly newspaper column.

"How does it feel as you enter your 90's to know that your generation used up one of the great aquifers of our planet?" Self-righteousness, sadly typical of many environmentalists, dripped off my words as I questioned my mother and friend.

"Don't forget, William, your education came from that irrigated land, so you don't get off scot-free. It's easy for you to judge the people you grew up with. We just didn't know any better. We thought the water would last forever. We wanted the good things it could provide."

She paused as if drifting off to decisions made long ago and forgotten but nudging into the moment.

"Even so, I feel terrible. In our wildest imagination we never thought we would use it up. It seemed so plentiful. Now, my grandchildren will not have the benefit of that land, nor will you in your old age. What will you do about this question of water?" She held me in the gaze of her mirthsome yet bold eyes, not letting me off the hook.

Our discussion about the weekly column continued and included lively exchanges. We lamented that her generation could not postpone its gratification for even one generation, much less for seven generations as the Iroquois elders taught.

> *"In our every deliberation we must consider the impact of our decisions on the next seven generations."*
>
> Iroquois Confederation

Neither can ours. We will see in Chapter 3 how the very survival of the human species now looms as an issue. The dry springs of my boyhood prophesied our current state, though I couldn't see it at the time. It was the canary in the coalmine. Such a circumstance pushes us to lean into critical questions if we are to merit the name we gave ourselves—***homo sapiens, wise men (people)***.

I see these burning questions in my grandchildren's eyes and on the tip of their tongues when I teach them to blow the conch shell to call us into Sacred Council. If it was difficult for my mother to face me with the reality of her generation's draining dry the precious aquifer, think what it will be like for us to look into our grandchildren's eyes and tell them we were the ones who made theirs the last generation of humans to see fresh water flow freely. Already one third of China has turned into a desert. Can the Southwest of our beloved continent be far behind?

> *"I measure the quality of the questions I ask, by the number to which I have no answer."*
>
> Albert Einstein

Here are the questions:

- Where would we be today without the breakthrough in consciousness that appeared through the discovery of music in the conch?
- What force drives and pulls evolution? What or Who is the Grand Attractor?
- Do we cover our heads with denial—the dominant defense of our culture?
- Will we drop off a precipice like driven buffalo crushing the hopes of the 200,000 year human experiment?
- Can we break our addiction to fossil fuels and extravagant life styles?
- Will we be accountable for our profligate habits?
- What possibility and hope does this grand moment in our human story hold?
- Who will step forward with the courage, awareness, choices, and practices to mentor us through the current Earth trauma?
- Will we be able to pass the torch to the next generation in good conscience, knowing we have done all we can do? Can we live and die in peace without that knowledge?
- Is there an untamed self inside who can counsel us in these challenging circumstances?

As we lean into these questions, a proposal arises. Not answers necessarily, but possibilities.

When all the trees have been cut down,
When all the animals have been hunted,
When all the waters are polluted,
When all the air is unsafe to breathe,
Only then will you discover you cannot eat money.

Bear Heart, quoting a Cree prophecy, as we sat by a stream, 1983

3

The Proposal

Turn now to a set of proposals, pointing to a path through Earth's current and unprecedented trauma.

Proposal #1

Our biggest problem is we think we have no problem.

In my four decades of practicing psychotherapy, I never cease to marvel at a curious human characteristic: our capacity for denying the reality before our very eyes. Countless times I have sat with families or organizations devastated by a variety of addictions, only to see the people adopt a view of reality denying the very addiction destroying them at every turn.

Therapists call the destructive addiction in the family system, the elephant in the room.

People still believing in a flat earth, in a government conspiracy lying to us about space travel to the moon, and in a scientific fabrication of the environmental crisis most likely aren't interested in looking inward to face the elephants of addiction and compulsions.

Yet, this inner journey is exactly where we need to go to wrestle with the pachyderm of denial.

What addiction are we denying at the root of the planetary crisis, as well as our personal suffering?

What is the elephant in the room of the human family?

Proposal #2

We are addicted to a life style outrageously beyond our means. Our decadent habits now place our species on the endangered list.

In his jolting article, *Why We Are All Addicted*, Andrew Weil, M.D. social observer and prominent physician, states: "The roots for predicted, global catastrophes go deep into the soil of addictive behavior. The world population increases grow in the soil of addictive and compulsive sex. The destruction of rainforests and the pollution of oceans and atmospheres flourish in the addiction to power and money. *The subject of addiction cannot be removed from the context of the possible end of life as we know it.*"[1]

These addictive impulses link with our many compulsions to create an extremely vulnerabe environment for the human project. eneath the crisis in civilization lies our role in Nature. We don't stand apart from Nature. We are an aspect of the natural order— the rising sun, gravity, pollination, photosynthesis, and weather patterns. *We are the environmental crisis*. We are Nature being aware of Herself in turmoil at this moment, unless we cover our eyes with rose-colored glasses.

Our human awareness is a powerful gift, and the epic of the human story demands we use this awareness to break through the massive denial. It is difficult to accept, but we humans are a destructive tendency in Mother Earth. Earth's immune system seeks to correct the malignancy we have become. As Nobel biologist, Rene Dubois, puts it, "From outer space our cities look like cancer cells."[2]

The elephant in the room is our
disturbance within Nature.

If you can't see the elephant in the room, can you at at least smell peanuts?

A mother heard of my work with young men and called about her son. He was fourteen, overweight, down on himself, depressed, and addicted to electronics and junk food. I told her I would be glad to see her son in an introductory interview. I made clear some of my guidelines. I have retired from psychotherapy, so what I do is eco-spiritual mentoring. She didn't know what that meant, so I explained. You bring your son to our land. We walk in the canyons and on the roads through the limestone hills. We will start slow, but eventually he will need to walk at least two hours carrying a back pack.

She was shocked. She didn't think he could do that much. If he could, what good would it do? What good is the simple act of walking and learning how to pay attention in a Nature outing? How could this help her son? How could it break through the fog of adolescence? How could this process cure depression and obesity? To her credit and to his, they were both willing to trust me enough to experiment. We walked. We talked. We looked at turkey eggs. We contemplated a snake. We sweated. We sat under the shade of a small tree on a hot Texas day. We nursed blisters on our feet. We developed a primal trust in moving close to Nature, in our relationship, and in all the creatures we encountered. We trusted that Nature wanted us to be better, to awaken to our true natures, to be aware. We learned the simple joy of an elder mentoring a young person.

A year passed. We walked some days for four hours. I told him it was impossible to walk in the wilds and stay depressed. He laughed but agreed. Soon, he approached age seventeen, and I, seventy. Now, he is at the University studying environmental science. He found his Wild Heart, and now he wants to do something about Earth's crisis. He made the quantum leap from wrestling with his personal crisis (borderline obesity and depression) to similar issues with the planet-at-large.

The mother, son, and I share a story with current humanity.

We must, then, find a path from the edge of the hurricane of our current dilemma, through the storms, into the still point of the eye. The storms buffet and scare us as we journey. About the time we make progress, we lose our courage and retreat to the outer edges of the hurricane. Frightened, we stay at the edge comforting ourselves with our compulsive life styles , pretending we aren't in a category four storm.

> *"I like to play indoors better 'cause that's where all the electrical outlets are."*
>
> A fourth grader speaking to Richard Louv, author and Expert on Nature-deficit Disorder

As the Earth's weather and climate are getting more and more rambunctious, superficial contact with Nature will not do. We have to become wilder, closer to the wisdom of our animal natures. To find our way through to survive and to thrive, we will have to move well beyond the confines of air-conditioned and computer-generated Nature. We will have to give up crucial elements of our usual control and allow the non-human elements of the Sacred Web to connect with us.

Proposal #3

The Web of Life, Mother Earth, wants to heal the cancer we humans have become. Once we break through our capacity to deny our profligate ways, She can begin expanding our ability to see our way through the morass. As we transform our own addictions, we position ourselves to become solutions to Earth's crisis.

What is Earth's hidden strategy for moving through the crisis? Is it technology? Alternative energy? Extended intelligence through computers and the internet? Meditation? Integral theories? A new spirituality brave enough to face overpopulation? Military and police upgrades? Learning survival skills? Reform of democracy? Better health care? Breakthrough psychology? Alternative universities?

All of these may eventually come into play, but first things first.

Proposal #4

Earth's unprecedented crisis reveals itself with the basics of the environment. Deep Nature herself is upset; therefore, we must return to the loins of Mother Nature. We must re-establish the primal connection. That is our first order of business. No significant solutions will arise without the nurturing of this connection with the mysterium tremendum, that profound sense of awe we feel lying on the Earth looking at the night sky. I refer here not to an occasional peak experience but to radical new practices to recover the Wild Heart birthed in Mother Nature's womb.

Proposal #4.5

We have lost our root connection to the Earth (root chakra). Only by descending to our roots can we grow a new Earth.

Even though it is important to break through the denial, I promise you, reader, I will not belabor a doomsday looming on the horizon. I trust you have been beaten about the head enough on this subject. The Divine judgment of the consequences of our own human behavior already confronts us. We will look at some of these bare bone facts staring us in the face in the next chapter.

Meditative thoughts for our jouney:

> *Within the deep resonance of the great unborn inside us, you can hear the sound of the sacred conch. You can hear the hidden truth of your very essence, your soul. You, in this moment and in every moment, abide as Spirit itself.*
>
> *This sound brings forth an immutable radiance beyond the immense suffering now loose on our planet. The Wild Heart of the Uncontrolled Mystery calls you through this sound. It speaks:*
>
> *Come deeper. Move from the edges. Listen to the rain on the roof. Step out of your house and feel the fierce blizzard on your skin. Walk along the street as you did as a child, feeling the splash of rain water on your face and filling up your shoes.*
>
> *I have but one secret for you today. I whisper in your ear as your mind quietens with the last light of day. Then, the sounds of night in tree frogs blend with cicadas to form my own music, our music, the music we have known before there was a homo sapiens, before the Universe itself was born.*
>
> *This magic sound of the spheres calls you to awaken.*
> *Awaken, my Beloved, to this moment.*
> *It is your moment.*
> *Our Love is our only hope.*
> *This is my Sacred Council.*

4

The Awakening

A circle of Homo sapiens gathers around a fire on an early Saturday morning in limestone hills. A cold rain challenges us to start the fire, and we wonder why we are outside shivering, not in bed. Some of us are Wisdom University faculty and students, others from an eco-spiritual group called the Earthtribe. We are here. We hunger for something.

> Hungry for what?
> Our hidden wilderness?
> The Mystery within and without?

A man in his early twenties muscles into the circle. He is new and introduces himself as Adam. The words on his faded tee shirt are barely readable: S.O.S. From a distance we all assume the letters refer to an Austin environmental movement called *Save Our Springs*. The organization aims at protecting the water in the springs of the Texas Hill Country aquifer vulnerable to human development. Upon closer examination we strain our eyes to see the dim message is something else quite beyond but related to saving the local springs. Is it an apocalyptic warning? Is it the sound of the conch shell in tee shirt form? We look closer to decipher its message.

Save Our Species, it reads.

Later in the day, as we eat a ceremonial meal, we laugh at the irony of a young man named Adam bringing us a message about the threat to the survival of our species, *Homo sapiens*. Is it the garden myth amped up? Are we now falling out of the garden totally into the abyss of extinction?

In the months that follow we dialogue about what we can do to save our species from extinction. Where is the apple of awareness when we need it most? What kind of awakening do we need? Is the conch calling through the tee shirt to wake us up before it is too late?

The tee shirt, the conch, and a garden variety of stirrings reach out to shake us awake. Let's explore these awakenings.

Awake to Our Moment

Once, Buddha's contemporaries asked him if he was a god. He thought for a moment and replied, "No, I am awake!" That was Gautama's moment, his moment to be the Buddha. This moment is ours! To save our species we need a ground swell of awakening. And it is happening.

Hungry for what? To awaken to our moment in the 200,000 year story of Homo sapiens on this beloved planet, Earth. Just as my foreparents blew the conch shell to awaken to the dangers and possibilities of the Texas frontier, so Earth's immense conch sends forth a blast to awaken us to this moment. Can you hear the polar ice breaking up? The volcanoes erupting? The earthquakes trembling?

Awake to the Wild Heart of Nature

We warmed our hands at the fire that cold morning because of a profound stirring in our human hearts to touch the Wild Heart of Nature. Shuﬄing our feet to stay warm, we aspired to be touched by that aspect of Nature not controlled by humans.

- Our classroom was the out-of-doors.
- Our church, the trees.
- Our therapy group, all living things.
- Our meditation, opening with breathing to the Natural Process.

To awaken we descend the spiral of evolution to the era when humans warmed their hands with fire. Our hominid ancestors have circled around fires for at least 790,000 years, as evidenced by charred wood and seeds in an archeological site in Israel[1]. Our forbearers smelled of smoke, felt the wind, and touched each other's shoulders. We seek to reclaim our heritage. We give up our beds and air conditioned space in order to connect with the part of ourselves lost in traditional, modern, and post-modern culture.

We know to save our species we have to return to those unbridled moments when humans knew they were a species among species, an animal among animals. We discover that no amount of education or fear concerning the climate crisis can help without the awakening of our primordial beings, our Paleolithic selves.

High-minded spiritual pathways that focus on ascending to altered and elevated states are not adequate in a global crisis of Mother Earth. Indoor mystical pathways have their place, but they are not sufficient for this hinge of history. They offer a Sacred Council of sorts, but such is not adequate for our day. Our path must take us into the roots of the undomesticated and passionate, the loins of the Earth.

In short, the smoking fire and conch call us to transform our relationship with Nature by rediscovering our shamanic traditions. When we embrace the indigenous dimension of ourselves, we know *we are an aspect of Nature. We are the cells of Mother Earth. We are Her awareness reflecting on the meaning of our recklessly prodigal ways. We are her aspect reaching beyond denial to the hope of new practices and habits.*

> **An old friend listened to stories of our students whose lives had been transformed by contact with the wild in Nature. With a wistful look in her eyes, she said,"I love everything about your work. I would love to be part of it, but I don't like bugs; I don't like sweat; I just don't like going outdoors that much. Is there any way to do this work without getting overheated and ruining my nails?"**

Awake to the Global Crisis

Such powerful moments of awe prepare us to face emerging reality. We have to confront our current life conditions. Without drama and hysteria the best of modern science tells us:

- CO_2 is out-of-control.
- Methane gas is not far behind as the tundra melts.
- Climate warming produces prodigious storms.
- Over population of our species is a root cause.
- Sea levels are rising.
- Forests, our planet's lungs, are disappearing.
- Our water practices put us at risk.
- Our cities are polluted.
- Our oceans struggle with plastic gyres the size of Texas.
- Viability of fish as a food source is tentative.
- The human ecological footprint is crucial.
- Our lack of awareness is the sword hanging over our heads.
- If we don't act swiftly, extinction of humans is in the picture.

In the previous chapter I promised I would not dwell on our self-destructive patterns. With that promise in mind, let's be as objective as possible. If you are suspicious of the environmental data supporting the above comments, check with the most conservative state university in your area. See what the scientists as a group are saying on this subject. In our area Texas A&M is moderate to conservative; it is home to the George Bush Presidential Library. Our very conservative Governor, Rick Perry, was a yell leader there, and he now appoints board members. With those conservative credentials in hand, the atmospheric science faculty at Texas A&M, nevertheless, has stated that the climate is clearly warming and humans have an important role.[2]

Awake to the Bigger Story

Run the video story back 200,000 years to the moment Homo sapiens walked across the bridge of evolution from human-like creatures to humans with all the equipment we have today.

Geneticists tell us the DNA trail leads us back to one woman in East Africa. Biologists call her the mitochondrial Eve. All 6.6 billion humans on the planet today owe her an expression of gratitude. For what? For awakening to her moment, for making choices, for developing her awareness, for giving birth to our species. She heard the call. She mentored the spiral of evolution through her choices. Without her sacred leadership we would not be here today. She reached deep inside her own shadows and doubts to find a hopeful aspect. She listened to the deeper essence. She was close to her Wild Heart. Out of her Sacred Council emerged Homo sapiens. She is our biological mother.

Appreciate the Last Monumental Crisis: 1000 Mating Pairs

Then, run the video story ahead to the 70,000 year mark. Africa is beset with droughts lasting over a hundred years. Geologic activity warms the climate. The atmosphere becomes heavy with volcanic eruptions. Humans fight with each other over scraps of nourishment and water. Finally, the human population is reduced to 1000 mating pairs. Yikes! Environmental pressure threatens to snuff out the human experiment.

We teeter on the brink of extinction. A moment of expanded awareness occurs. A small group sees through the crisis and beyond. They don't have to die with their limited views. Like the mitochondrial Eve, they open themselves to a larger story. They don't have to perish in their small world. Picture in your mind's eye a circle of elders in council considering their options. They reach a decision to start the great journey: the planetary migrations out of Africa. Pause for a moment. Give thanks to this small group who heeded the call of the beyond. They went forth and multiplied. We need to go forth and reduce our numbers. What spiritual framework will emerge with the value of compassionate population reduction?

Time and again, our species comes to a crossroads, usually precipitated by a climate crisis. Each time, as a species, we have come through stronger, more aware, and more able to work with an increasingly complex universe through aware choices and novel practices. Our possibilities during our current trauma arise when we realize the vast potential in Nature's creation of the human spirit.

What we face now is indeed unique because the human species currently creates the crisis, or at the very least, participates in a tipping point in the environmental trauma. With that said, our potential is unlimited. We simply must not be paralyzed by our despair at the enormity of the challenge or by sticking our heads in the sand.

The DNA of the 1000 mating pairs runs through us, telling us, "You can do this thing. We did it. So can you. We sat in Sacred Council with ourselves and each other and decided to make the great journey. So can you."

Awake to the Apex of Evolution

Recently, Ken Burns produced a television series called *The National Parks: America's Best Idea*. He pictures John Muir journeying into the Wild Heart of Yosemite, being touched and awakened to new levels of awareness. Muir realizes if he doesn't act quickly America's wild areas will disappear. Soon, Enos Mills joins the movement to establish a National Park in Colorado. Stephen Mather, a retired capitalist, camps on a mountain side and notices a swelling sense of awe. He throws all his wealth and energy into the project and becomes the first head of the National Parks system.

Incredibly, this dream of protecting the wild for the public had never dawned on humans before. 200,000 years had passed, and for the first time a nation sets aside public land for meditative possibilities and play for its people. There were no National Parks in ancient Greece or in historic Europe. None existed at the time of Muir in Central or South American. None could be found in Siberia, or Russia. This small cadre, perhaps a dozen at the most, gave birth to an idea that saved the Wild for the planet's people. All the National Parks of the globe stem from this seed group of Americans awakening to a new awareness, a new consciousness, new choices, and, most important, active and novel practices.

They were the apex of evolution at that moment. Intuitively, they knew humans had to rediscover their indigenous minds in the depths of Nature if they were to survive and thrive. Nature calls us to be that apex of consciousness in this day.

Awake to Eco-Evolutionary Consciousness

What kind of consciousness do we need to save our species? What form of consciousness is awakened near the Loins of Mother Earth? To unfold the quality of consciousness needed in this massive transition, we will need to embrace the interplay of our inner world with the Earth. I will explore this form of consciousness in greater depth in Parts II and III.

Here are some bare bones to launch our discussion:

- We need to be aware of a sub-self which denies our crisis. (More about sub-selves in Part II)
- We must listen to our sub-self of denial but not be dominated by it.
- We also must access the Wild Heart sub-self, the key player in the current crisis.
- That accomplished, we go to the vision mountain and learn to witness the activity of our personal and cultural ego. The witness consciousness brought forth by new connections with The Untamed Infinity of Nature gives us perspective.
- We can't stop there. Next, we take that visionary consciousness from the mountain back into our usual operating ego.
- Now the ego collaborates with the witness of the higher place. It couples with our new awareness to form an aware ego, born of non-dual consciousness.
- This aware ego allows us to make choices to survive and thrive in this crucial moment.
- Out of these choices arise practices that reduce our ecological footprint. Walking lightly with fewer demands on the planet is the strong first step to take us away from the brink.

These bare bones offer the frame of a strong body for our life crises. They offer the first substantial step in the journey through our current life conditions. They point us in the direction of our Sacred Inner Council.

Awake and Act With 80/20

With Wisdom University (wisdomuniversity.org) and State of the World Forum we join in the bold aspiration and practice of reducing our ecological footprint by 80% by 2020. We begin with ourselves, our own consciousness, our own choices, and our own practices. We, the people, can do this. We can no longer depend on our governments primarily to act for us. This is our moment to step up.

Our political leaders, in my estimation, are captured by the current system. The Kyoto and Copenhagen Accords only underline their unwillingness to step into this moment. Our hope lies in the Nature-based circles drawing on the deeper wisdom of the Wild Heart. These grass-roots Sapiens Circles teem with creativity and energy. They will provide us with a platform of safety and creativity and inform leaders at a global level.

Awake and Pass the Fire of Our Consciousness

Now, run the time video to 28,000 years ago to a cave in Gibraltar. A small band of our genetic cousins, the Neanderthals, gathers round a fire similar to the one described at the beginning of this essay, the fire where we first saw the tee shirt, S.O.S. The Neanderthals had larger brains than we current humans. They were stronger. They conserved heat better than we humans do. Yet, their numbers had been reduced to a last handful.

Why? A warming climate? An inability to form co-operative communities that could drive protein over cliffs? Contraction into family groups to the exclusion of a larger community? Seduced by their own small stories? Lack of physical and mental flexibility? Limited self awareness and expression? Little or no art? Lost touch with the subtleties of natural cycles? Devotion to traditional habits? Denial about their vulnerability? Failure of a visionary,inner council?

They warm their hands with the fire in what is now called Gorham's Cave. One last time they lie down to sleep. The next morning, outside the cave the unmistakable smell of rosemary rides the wind into the cave and circles around the now ebbing fire. Plentiful wild asparagus waits to nourish them. Yet, none of the Neanderthals wakes up that morning. Their species will never again wake to the morning Sun. They will never eat again of the Earth's bounty. They are the last of their kind. Their fire has gone out. Their species sleeps forever.

What about our fire? The one we humans have lost but now hope to find? Are we here? Are we done? Do we vibrate with hope? Run the time video forward to the 7th generation in the future. Wise, indigenous elders urge us on to join our hands and voices to answer these questions for our children's children.

> *"Let us put our minds together and see what kind of life we can make for our children."*
>
> Sitting Bull, 1877

Today, let us make a sacred vow to seven generations ahead of us:

We will not allow the human fire to go out.
We will survive and thrive as humans, a specie among species.
We will wake up.

Don't go back to sleep.
Don't go back to sleep.
Don't go back to sleep.

Having considered my proposals and awakened to the sound of the conch, we now turn to beginning maps to guide us through the storms. We begin with ourselves, knowing such examination provides the source of profound change. I propose a seismic shift in consciousness once we notice our inner council and connect with the sublime and wild, long repressed.

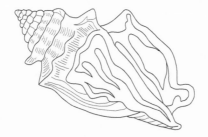

PART II

The Sacred Council Gathers

"We are joined to one another by awareness, and, in our di⊠ering selves, we manifest our uniqueness and di⊠erences in relation to one another."

— Hal and Sidra Stone,
Embracing Our Selves

"I am one powerful self made up of so many selves that sometimes I throw myself a get-acquainted party."

— Eric Maisel

"Using inner-family councils: All personality sub-selves agree on comfortable, safe outer and inner places to meet."

— Peter K. Gerlach, *Inner Councils*

"...there are many parts of your being, many personalities, each acting on its own behalf and in its own way."

— Sri Aurobindo,
Our Many Selves: Practical Yogic Psychology

5

Roots of the Sacred Council

On June 11, 1776, the Continental Congress counseled concerning the issue of how individual colonies related to each other. Could they form a union? Sensing the need for mentoring, they invited Iroquois elders to sit with them. Heated debate stirred the participants as they considered how the parts (colonies) related to the Greater Whole (a possible nation). Their dialogue was fueled by the burden of taxation without representation. Little did the Colonists know a fierce winter lay ahead to compound the trauma of revolutionary war.

Thomas Jefferson, John Adams, John Hancock, and Ben Franklin were all familiar with the Iroquois Confederacy. As early as 1744, Franklin sat in council with the Indigenous Confederacy and marveled at how six tribes could govern an area that stretched from Ohio through the Great Lakes to upper New York. A respected elder, Canassatego, impressed Franklin with his wise demeanor. When the Colonial governors assembled in council at Lancaster, Pennsylvania, they asked for his wisdom in order to ground themselves, given the turbulent times.

Canassatego spoke: "We are a powerful Confederacy. By your observing the methods our wise forefathers have taught us, you will acquire strength and power. Whatever befalls you, never fall out with one another."[1]

These were simple words, yet the energy and democratic model of the indigenous elders stayed with Franklin for thirty-two years. The June gathering in 1776 weighed heavily on Franklin's mind. He didn't know if he, Jefferson, and Adams could bring together these various colonies and forge a whole. He was worried. In that frame of mind, he sought Iroquois wise persons once again to offer council at this very important moment in the birthing of a nation. The Declaration of Independence seemed as out of the question as big minded co-operation between Democrats and Republicans and peace in the Middle East are today.

The Native council's roots, argue some anthropologists, reach as far back as 1100 CE, a time when Europe was mired in the Dark Ages. Furthermore, the Iroquois Confederacy is arguably the oldest living participatory democracy on Earth since it is still effectively functioning. The profound wisdom of their council provided a matrix of consciousness important to the forming of America's young nation, as we shall see.

A crucial turning point in the Founding Father's deliberation came with the indigenous consciousness of an Iroquois elder, whose name is lost in history. He stood and speaking with a clear voice invited a friendship between the emerging nation and the Iroquois Confederacy that would "last as long as the sun shines and the waters run."

Next, in the council came a ceremony. We don't know the extent of the ceremony, but we do know the representative of the Iroquois Council gave John Hancock, the first signer of the Declaration of Independence, a Nature-based name. I can imagine the wise elder unwrapping the Sacred conch shell and belting out a robust sound that reverberated throughout the meeting hall. In my mind the elder takes the shell respectfully in hand along with a Sacred Pipe and touches Hancock on his third eye and his heart. He speaks, "For the next leg of the journey, for the good of our Grandmother, the Earth, I give you the name: *Karanduawn* or *The Great Tree*."[2]

And so it came to be: the first signer of the Declaration of Independence, John Hancock, was guided by *The Great Tree* and was known by this Nature-based name in intimate moments to Jefferson, Adams, and Franklin.[3] This grand ceremonial event is eerily reminiscent of scenes from the movie *Avatar*, which I will discuss in Chapter 14.

If the United States could recover the spiritual energy of that moment for our time, we would go a long way down the road to being a Sacred Mentor for the current trauma of the Earth. We could truly be an ecological leader, not just in military or economic power but also in depth of wisdom. We could give up our Empire status and take on the mantle of The Great Tree. We could remember our roots. Herein is an alternative power source full of possibility. We could point the nations (sub-divisions) of the Earth toward a larger Confederacy (Global Whole).

In the vein of building a metaphor between the early nation and our personal, inner council, the content of the words offered by the Indigenous elders is not as important as their primordial presence and quiet integrity. They brought a form of natural awareness essential to the founding fathers and, indeed, all humans. Unfortunately, these founding fathers were men—and I emphasize men—who missed several crucial elements available in the Iroquois' energetic presence.

For example, we could ask: why did they give Hancock a Nature name? *John Hancock* is the name of the operating ego, the usual configuration of selves. But the Iroquois saw something deeper in Mr. Hancock. They saw his essence, his soul. To emphasize that deeper identity they gave his essence a name, an indigenous practice throughout the planet. In doing so, they invited the Wild Heart of the forest to sit in the circle of his inner council, thus giving it the potential of a Sacred Council. This gift of a name must have seemed strange to these men of European extraction since they were baptized with a Christian name they kept throughout their lives. More questions arise. Did Hancock and the young nation follow the guidance of these Indigenous elders? How does this story relate to the forming of our inner councils to face our crises?

Using this historical incident as a beginning place, this section of the book explores the interplay of the inner Sacred Council and its influence on the exterior world. I have used the term *Sacred Council* many times thus far. I have pointed in the direction of its meaning. It is now time to get down to the business of further exploring the meaning of this phrase by looking at an arrangement within every human I am calling a *council of selves*.

6

The Inner Council of Selves

Like the early colonies our inner world holds many sub-divisions. I call them sub-selves, or simply selves. The Iroquois League contained six sub-divisions which formed a unity. In a major miracle of historical proportions, the thirteen colonies also forged a unity. Apply this process to our inner universe. Our interior world contains many more than thirteen aspects. A few of the common selves are: the inner critic, the pleaser, the perfectionist, the victim, the persecutor, the pusher, and the rescuer. Our inner development parallels the development of the colonial sub-divisions; like them, we need a centralized, organizing force.

In the case of a young nation, Jefferson's colony, Virginia, thought organizing its own colony was the priority, many times more significant than the

"A biography is considered complete if it merely accounts for six or seven selves, whereas a person may well have as many as a thousand."

Virginia Woolf

nation as a whole. Each of the thirteen colonies vied for center stage, lobbying for its own good, often forgetting the larger national story. (It is worth noting that these brilliant founding people rarely had a vision large enough to include the Earth as a whole.)

Sometimes these sub-divisions (individual colonies) even attempted to run the whole, dominated by their own small story and unaware of or, perhaps pushing aside, the unity attempting to arise in their midst. At other times—as in the Declaration of Independence—the parts co-operated with the larger whole and made a quantum leap up the evolutionary spiral to the bigger story, the national vision.

What happened to allow this quantum leap? Historians search for specific suggestions as an influence of the Iroquois League in the forming of the United States as a nation. In doing so, they miss the energetic context of wisdom offered by the League elders. We can't fault historians too much, for such Earth Wisdom is often a foundational thread, not visible to many, felt not seen.

What the League offered was not only ideas about consensus and participatory democracy but also **witness consciousness empowered by contact with Nature**. I will delve into the richness of this form of consciousness momentarily. It is enough now to state that the witness consciousness is a key element missing in addressing the current planetary crisis. Just as the Constitutional Congress needed the Earth Wisdom and grounding influence of the Iroquois, so we need a similar influence in our inner self-organization to bring our parts together into a wise whole.

Beginning Essentials for the Inner Sacred Council

What do we need for our own Sacred Council?

- Begin with these essentials: the wisdom of the elders and the witness consciousness.
- More specifically, we need Nature-based wisdom as exemplified by the Iroquois.
- Before we can have this form of consciousness in culture, we will need to develop it within our various inner councils.
- On a larger scale as a result of individual work, many circles around the planet are forming, using this emerging indigenous wisdom as a focal point.
- Out of this matrix of consciousness arise solutions to the current global crisis.

The Operating Ego: The Limits of Protection and Control

Here is my perception of the current condition of our inner world. We have a mass of inner sub-selves operating much of the time like a tangled glob of wiggling worms, akin to the unruly colonies just before the American Revolution. We lump our inner worlds together in this current condition to form a dominant, collective ego configuration known as the modern/postmodern, prevailing culture.

To shift metaphors, on the inner stage we have a group of sub-selves that grab center stage and run our lives. They dominate our inner world. Much of the time they actually think

> *"A council fire for all the nations shall be kindled. We will kindle it also for the seven nations living toward the sunrise, and for the nations that dwell towards the sunset. All shall receive the Great Law and labor together for the welfare of man.*
>
> Deganawidah, A Founder of the Iroquois Confederacy

they are who we are. The Buddhists call this condition—the monkey mind. I prefer to think of this condition of out-of-control, control.

Let me illustrate. Suppose I ask you what you think about global warming. If you are on the far right, you will likely answer: it is a hoax foisted on us by Al Gore. The voice speaking is not your deeper self but a protective set of selves who seek to protect and control through denying any real problem. Their job is to defend at all costs the wall of *truth* you believe in wholeheartedly.

If you are a moderate conservative, you will likely answer with thorough skepticism. The

> **Most of us live our lives in a case of a sad mistaken identity. Who we think we are is a tiny minority of our inward aspects. The biggest part of us is hidden.**

conglomerate of selves speaking for you seek to protect you by being skeptical about any data not supporting your safety and life style. Your skepticism is not so much based in data but in your fear of losing what is important to you. It is not the essential you speaking but the protective *you*, who seeks to control through skepticism and pessimism.

If you are a cultural creative on the far left, your set of selves that speak will have the certainty of a Christian evangelist or an Islamic fundamentalist. The complex of selves speaking at your inner microphone are certain you have the truth about global warming. There is no discussion. Your inner voices preach, "We are collapsing through global warming." You are not interested in dialogue, only convincing others of the danger. You speak from the high horse of certainty. Anyone who raises the smallest question is condemned by your set of selves to the purgatory of denial. "If you don't agree with me to the fullest degree, you are in denial." Such is your party line when you are dominated by this set of selves. They are not the essential you but the protective you, who seeks to save the planet by controlling the conversation.

If you are a cultural creative interested in complexity and dialogue, you will answer with a set of selves who basically see we are entering a planetary storm of unprecedented magnitude. However, you are open to new data about how this crisis will play out. You know Nature is full of surprises, and you don't claim to have all the truth. You recognize climate-warming data has been politicized and sometimes is not accurate.

In spite of your interest in personal growth, your operating ego most likely has not assisted you in opening up to the depths of Nature. You report about Nature rather than speaking from a deep awakening to Nature's Presence. Prolonged connection with Nature is too inconvenient and uncomfortable. Besides, you are busy saving the world. In short, you don't want your protection, comfort, and control challenged by the unpredictability of personal exposure to the wilds.

My point here is the *essential* you cannot fully flower until your inner council breathes fresh air. That flowering requires more than an occasional high you get from a nature outing; it demands an ongoing practice of connecting with the Sacred Web of Life in its raw form.

The various sets of selves addressing the planetary crisis have certain qualities in common.

- They want to protect you.
- They run on automatic
- They pay little attention to feedback.
- They view disagreement as destructive.
- They do whatever they need to do to protect you by controlling the environment.
- They tend to speak in sound bytes.
- They are estranged from the Wild Heart of Nature, which they see as a threat to their usual control of you and your life.
- They believe in their heart of hearts, they are YOU.

I call this set of inner selves *the operating ego*. I know I am in that operating state when I refuse to acknowledge the limits of power in whatever position I take.

Our situation is worse than Gandhi imagined. Everywhere our many i's go, our many i's go with us and seek solutions through protection and control of anything that threatens the status quo. The operating ego can then be defined as organized *protection and control.*

> *"Every where I go, I goes with me and I spoils everything."*
>
> Stanley Jones quoting Gandhi, personal conversation

This operating ego is not evil. We don't need to get rid of this configuration of inner selves. Calling the operating ego the *monkey mind* just makes this set of selves more determined to hold onto the inner microphone. They don't like to be called a name by some new spiritual kid on the block. We couldn't banish them even if we wanted to do so, because our organism has had considerable success being run by this operating ego. Despite this success, there is a big catch here: the wiggling mass of operating egos we call *culture* has driven the collective human auto into a ditch.

So, we need to do something with our operating egos, but what? My proposal is that we create an inner council on a personal level similar to the one our founding fathers created on a national level. Or, going closer to the Wild Heart of Nature, I actually prefer the Iroquois Council to early American democracy. The Indigenous Council was a *Sacred Council* because they were more inclusive of various aspects of themselves and the tribes.

A strong hint as to what made the Iroquois council sacred lies in Plato's comment about the human endeavor as being the *enlargement of the soul*. For the council to be sacred the personal story needs to get larger and larger, the vision wider and wider.

> Your present moment—whatever it is—will have to find its place against the backdrop of the 200,000 year human story. This moment is not all about you. It is about us—all of us, humans and non-humans.

To enlarge our discussion, let's invite several sets of sub-selves to sit in the council. We need to open our council and to enlarge our inner dialogue. The founding fathers invited the Iroquois elders, so we can invite hidden, inner resources as well. Be aware of this reality: our usual operating egos do their best to take care of the vulnerable selves they know about, but most of our vulnerability lies outside our usual awareness. These vulnerable selves lie hidden from our usual activities. They languish in the wings of the inner stage, in the shadows beyond the spotlight. We keep them in the back seat and sometimes in the trunk of our car.

The next phase of our discussion moves to the back seat to see what we can do with hidden vulnerabilities. Therein lies a direction for moving through our crises.

7

The Hidden Vulnerable Selves

Hidden from our view is our massive collection of vulnerable selves. They tremble with fear at the thought of the world falling into chaos with one environmental catastrophe after another, collapse around the corner, not to mention everyday vulnerabilities like illness, economic stress, relationship strife, and leaks in the roof.

This past year I spent considerable time with global teachers, wise elders with whom I rub elbows in my work with Wisdom University. What I noticed was our mutual struggle to own our hidden vulnerability about the planetary crisis. I heard angry sub-selves, railing with prophetic zeal against the indifference of our culture regarding the environmental crisis. I heard righteous selves pointing at corporate and governmental villains. I heard brilliant diagnostic selves. I saw social artistry selves and sacred activist selves creatively at work. I observed all of these sub-selves in others and myself, but nowhere did I encounter the vulnerable.

I understand. It is easier to be in the operating ego than to listen to and feel the hidden, vulnerable selves. I have yet to observe myself, or other environmentalists for that matter, say with tender, frail voices, "I am just scared out of my wits by our current situation. I am at a loss. I don't know what to do."

Instead of bringing these vulnerable selves into the council circle, our operating egos attempt to protect the status quo through a variety of control measures, compulsions, and reactive addictions. Automatically and without awareness our operating egos rant with voices of anger, self-righteousness, rationality, judgment, criticism, and, most of all, stress-filled activity. We mistakenly believe if we just work hard enough, we will feel better.

What does it mean to bring the vulnerable selves into Sacred Council? It means we pass them the talking stick (or, to use a current metaphor, the microphone in the board room) and allow them to speak without interruption,

- without calling them stupid or uninformed,
- without seeing them as victims,
- without rescuing them,
- without criticizing them as being in denial.

In short, pulling in our vulnerabilities means we listen to them within the safe container of the Sacred Council. It means we develop an awareness large enough to discover the kernel of truth embedded in the vulnerable voices. It means we refrain from covering them over with angry, critical, and self-righteous voices.

If you look around at the variety of tools we use in our dominant culture to handle vulnerability, you will discover we use hammers when we actually need paint brushes. If you feel frightened and vulnerable about our world conditions, then you can—according to the messages all around us—take a medication for erectile dysfunction or depression, visit the local mall, sit at the bar, find a drug dealer, search for spectacular sex, invest in an upbeat stock, start a war, bail the big boys out, find a tea party, engage in plastic surgery, or follow the latest public drama. We try nearly anything to avoid sitting with our inner vulnerability.

Do you recall what our then President suggested when we were devastated by 9-11? Be calm and continue shopping. Somehow, that strategy was supposed to take care of how shaken we were. It didn't.

What I propose is a deep listening to these vulnerabilities in a conversation with our sub-selves in such a way they can feel safe and offer us feedback for our journey.

First, we must summon the courage to face a whole other class of sub-selves—the inner shadows, who also reside in the wings of our inner stage. Our vulnerable selves are never as frightened as when we refuse to do our shadow work.

8

The Shadow Selves

The shadow selves are aspects of our inner life pushed into the dark recesses of our interior by our usual operating egos. We disown these selves because these shadow aspects are not acceptable to the values we hold or the patterns of our lives. These sub-divisions of ourselves live in the darkness, of our unconscious, also known as the subconscious.

Imagine for a moment an inner council circle with a talking stick being passed around, as practiced by the Iroquois Council even to this day. In the Indigenous world, the talking stick is passed with each person in the circle having the opportunity to talk while holding the stick. The remainder of the circle listens without interruption until the stick completes the circle as one person finishes talking and passes it to the next person.

The status quo participants enjoy the warmth of a nice fire in the center of the circle, and the conversation unfolds brilliantly until a commotion of voices from outside the circle yell at the top of their lungs in an effort to be heard. The circle itself continues with the conversation, but the voices outside the circle become louder and louder.

Finally, one of the selves from the shadows bursts into the circle, kicks at the fire, upsets the equilibrium, and yells in our face.

At that point we can either invite the shadow self to take a seat in the circle or banish it once again. In order for the Council to be Sacred, we will need to find a way to bring the shadow selves into the council and allow them to speak, preferably in a safe way.

If we don't offer a seat to the shadow selves in the council, then they will eventually cause all kinds of mischief in our lives. Go back for a moment to the Founding Fathers in 1776. They excluded minorities and women from their council. This exclusion reflected their own inner council, including their values that white men should run the world. In that sense the founding council was not sacred.

> *"The only devils in this world are those running around inside our own hearts, and that is where all our battles should be fought."*
>
> Gandhi,
> quoted in *Wildlife Federation*, May-June, 1997

Our participatory democracy has been limited by the exclusion of the shadow voices of the Divine Feminine from the inner council of the founding fathers. When I use the term Divine Feminine I refer to the values, beliefs, and practices of the Indigenous peoples of the world as exemplified by the Iroquois. We shall soon explore how the Wild Heart and the Divine Feminine are closely related.

Occasionally, the founding fathers listened to Abigail Adams. They could not ignore her brilliance. But that was about it for women. Oh, yes, we learned in American history Betsy Ross sewed the first American flag, though scholars now tell us such an account is a fable not rooted in history. The much-acclaimed founding fathers disowned the inner feminine and automatically disenfranchised the women of the emergent nation. In turn the

> **The truly Sacred necessitates inclusion; wholeness, not just preferred parts.**

sensitive and intuitive sides of ourselves became to a large extent *persona non grata* in our consciousness as an early nation.

This disowning of these valuable selves within would have devastating consequences for our planet and, eventually, ourselves.

Let's see how excluding parts—whether women or people of color—works out on a national level. Eighty-five years after the signing of the Declaration of Independence in 1776, the bloody War of the Rebellion erupted in 1861 over the exclusion of African slaves in the voting process. The abolitionist selves broke into the inner councils of many Americans and demanded to be heard; they would not be denied. It was an inner struggle manifesting on the national stage. Even after that terrible war, Abraham Lincoln could not bring himself to include Native Americans or women in the council, so they remained in the deep recesses of national consciousness for another fifty years.

In the historical world, wars follow upon wars; a major cause is the exclusion of key minorities we lock away in well-guarded prisons. Inner wars follow based on ongoing exclusion of shadow selves. History begins with our inner council. Generally, we have not fully included the feminine in our inner council, and that spells trouble for Earth's current crisis.

> Just as the nation still suffers from its propensity to exclude its shadows, so our inner world suffers when we exclude our shadows.

Jefferson, Adams, and Franklin did not include the inner shadows of their interior minorities and repressed the feminine in their council. So naturally they excluded these minorities from their decisions about who would have power in the new nation. These men were great, and we owe them gratitude. Yet, think what we might be like as a nation had they done their shadow work! To do so would have meant transcending the European values of their day; they weren't up to it. I regret to say I would probably have been right there with them.

Let's see how this council drama of shadow selves plays out with regard to the Earth's trauma in today's scene.

If you are an archconservative related to the environmental crisis, then you most likely push the wolf-at-the-door (catastrophe) out of the circle. You prefer to be with people who agree with you. If you awake to a cold day in the dead of winter, you mutter to anyone who will listen, "So much for global warming." You despise the inner self who might agree with Al Gore (or consensus science), so you push her out of your council.

If you are a moderate conservative and genuinely skeptical concerning the data indicating global warming, you most likely forcibly expel the parts of you looking at melting glaciers out of the circle. You move away from cities choked with pollution and read editorials railing against tree-huggers. Meanwhile, your inner tree hugger sings *Kum ba ya* at the edge of your council circle, but you won't let him have the microphone. Instead you make fun of tree huggers as the worst kind of societal offenders. If a mentor suggests that you have a Nancy Pelosi inside wanting to be heard, you think the person a bit daft.

If you are a left-leaning cultural creative, your circle is as small as the arch conservatives. You make room only for those people who not only agree with you but also who show considerable disdain toward those who don't. If a mentor or friend suggests to you that you have an inner Sarah Palin wanting the microphone inside yourself, you would think the suggestion inane, or, worse, an indication that the mentor herself was in denial merely for suggesting an embracing of your shadow Sarah. If some research suggests the possibility that 92% of the current global warming is due to so-lar activity, you consider the researcher disloyal to your cause. Your operating ego doesn't want data contrary to your position, so you push that data into the shadows. You become what at one time was your worst fear: a dogmatist.

> **Arch conservatives and closed-minded liberals alike run their lives on a transfusion of certitude. They have an IV stand rolling around dripping sound bytes into their arm. What close-minded archetypes reside within you? We all have them.**

If you are a more balanced cultural creative, your circle is a bit larger. However, you rarely talk to arch conservatives. If Rush Limbaugh or Sarah Palin invited you to dinner to discuss the evils of bleeding heart liberals, you would be sick to your stomach.

Your inner Rush and Sarah are not welcome in your inner council. If a mentor suggests you adopt the spiritual practice of making friends with a conservative, conversing regularly with said person, and listening with an open mind, you would find it very difficult.

Return to June, 1776. Our founding fathers forged a dominant culture. They called the Sacred Feminine into their council in the form of the Iroquois elders, but then they drove the elders out. They valued the Iroquois model but not enough to give the Indigenous people voting rights, or really any rights at all. In doing so they silenced access to their Wild Hearts.

Further, the Founding Fathers omitted the Iroquois Confederacy's practice of putting women in places of power. Women had the power to decide if the League went to war. They selected the chiefs. Had Jefferson, Adams, and Franklin brought this practice into the emerging nation, the course of the globe would have been very different. I am not holding the founding fathers to our current cultural standards but to values of their contemporaries, the so-called savages in the Iroquois Confederacy.

In a similar way we—with a few notable exceptions—have

Scientists estimate the population of Indigenous people in 1492 at 50 million. By the end of the War of 1812, 40 million Native Americans had died. Contrast that number with the horror of the Jewish Holocaust—six million. In 1864, outside Denver, a wagon train of American pioneers wiped out an entire peace-loving tribe after using the ruse of inviting them in for supper. The civilized citizens then hung the body parts of the so-called savages from the wagons as they traveled westward. No charges were ever brought against the perpetrators. Such atrocities were not uncommon. Abraham Lincoln was President. Civilization was pushing its primordial heart into the shadows with chilling efficiency, only to see it erupt in a twisted manner through such actions.

excluded the Sacred Feminine from our inner council of selves. The roots of the Sacred Feminine reside in the Nature-based selves, and we are estranged from this bountiful resource of creativity. They, too, dwell in the backseat as we motor down the road. It's getting pretty crowded back there with vulnerable selves, Nature-based or Wild Heart selves, and a plethora of other shadows.

When Judith and I were rearing our two daughters, Kris and Holly, we often took trips across country to National Parks in search of connecting with the Wild Heart. Along the way the two children in the back seat would get into mischief. Sometimes, one of the parents would turn around and say, "Don't make me stop this car." In all of our travels, I can recall only one time we actually stopped the car. That one time is still a top story at family gatherings. Stopping the car and facing unruly children in the backseat is not the adult idea of relaxation and vacation. To avoid a scene we threaten and keep on going. Usually, it leads to more mischief.

No council for the 21st Century can be Sacred without the luminosity of our Nature-based selves. Hope for our mounting crises means stopping and listening not only to the mischief but also to the luminosity. Let's see why.

9

The Nature-Based Selves:
Wild Heart

Thirty years ago I came in from a vision quest with the clear sense that all emotional and environmental problems stem from the act of shoving our more natural selves into the shadows. As a practicing psychotherapist, such a vision held immense importance for how I worked with clients. Within five years—in collaboration with my spouse, Judith Yost and others—I constructed a model of psychotherapy called ecodrama or ecotherapy. Numerous professional articles and books followed over the next decade, as I clarified for myself the implications of that vision.

"Nature-deficit Disorder: *Several studies suggest that thoughtful exposure of youngsters to nature can be a powerful form of therapy for attention-deficit disorder and other maladies. As one scientist puts it, we can now assume that just as children need good nutrition and adequate sleep, they may very well need contact with nature. If they don't have this exposure, they are likely to develop nature-deficit disorder, which has a number of personal and social symptoms.*

Richard Louv,
Last Child in the Woods, 2008

Briefly, here is how the process of embracing your nature-based selves works.

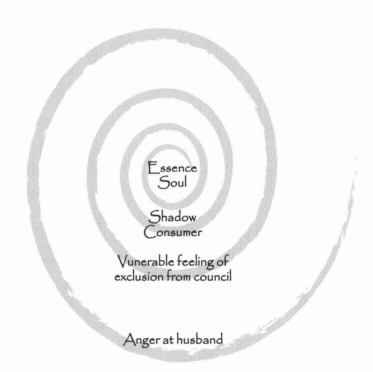

Let's say you are a woman who goes to an eco-spiritual mentor for help with anger you feel towards your husband and men in general. Your mentor takes you out-of-doors to a spiral circle drawn in freshly raked dirt. As you look at it, it reminds you of a weather photo of a hurricane system. Your mentor invites you symbolically to place your anger at the edge of this spiral and give it the microphone to voice itself. You listen to what your anger tells you, and you discover it is about not being heard by your husband and about "men who have basically turned the planet into an environmental trash heap."

Next, you move into another band of the spiral, a step closer to the center. Standing on this band within the spiral, you discover a vulnerability hiding underneath the anger. The vulnerable part of you is afraid you will not be included in the larger council of life. As a woman, you discover there are good reasons for this feeling, because our national process has systematically pushed women out of the cultural council. Most of all the vulnerable aspect is afraid it is too late to do anything about what the male-dominated world has done to the planet.

Your mentor invites you to look at what really disgusts you about men. You discover a shadow. What you hate about men is how they make everything answer to profit, command, control, and material wealth.

"Hmmm," your mentor queries, "Do you benefit from your husband's wealth?" Eventually, you discover your inner patriarch is a practicing capitalist, a hidden shadow within. You see your own methods of command and control. As you get to know this side of yourself, you sense freedom and energy. But where do you go now?

Interestingly enough, you now see another kind of shadow, the *golden shadow*. The dark shadow is that which you don't like in yourself, so you push it out of your consciousness. *The golden shadow is the immense possibility deep inside.* You keep it in the shadows because it might mean radical change in your life. It is the repression of the sublime potential resting within your soul. Let's inquire further.

Once again, you are out-of-doors with your mentor still standing in the spiral drawn on the ground, and she invites you to look around for help. You locate a beautiful oak tree and connect with it. The tree comforts you in some strange way. You find your mind full of memories from childhood when you climbed up into a tree house and when honey suckle tasted as good as it smelled. You feel peaceful. Like John Hancock, The Great Tree enters your inner council. Your mentor assists you in embracing this golden shadow—your natural inclination to bond with non-human species, indeed the biosphere.

You discover what Harvard biologist, E.O. Wilson, in his important book, *The Future of Life*, calls *biophilia, love of all life.*

> **The Golden Shadow:
> The Indigenous Self.**
> The way through our current planetary crisis emerges when we call a key golden shadow into our inner council. This golden shadow consists of a mysterious self full of potential, possibility, hope, and creativity. I refer to a self not dominated by current culture. It has been banished from our inner councils by our inner status quo. Just as President Lincoln refused to give the Indigenous people the right to vote, so we have refused our inner Indigenous self its rightful voice in our council. Now, is the time to listen to its counsel.

Your heart feels strangely warmed, then awakened and vibrant. You take off your shoes and feel the dirt under your feet in the spiral. You take off your shirt and let your skin breathe. If your mentor were not there, you would take off all your clothes and dance around the circle and howl like a wolf. You howl. Your mentor howls. You laugh. Your mentor laughs. You go back to your anger for a moment and growl. You picture your husband and growl at him. You think about the fact that your grandmother couldn't vote until much later in life. You growl at the system. You think about all of the trees being cut down. You growl. You are the voice of The Great Tree. You are embracing your Wild Heart self. Your anger subsides. Your mind clears and slows down.

These Nature-based selves are called forth by the wind in the trees, the dirt on the ground, the brilliance of sun reflecting off butterfly wings. They have been dormant inside. Open the windows. Turn off the air conditioning. Breathe deeply.

> *"Art attracts us only by what it reveals of our most secret self."*
> Alfred North Whitehead

The fresh air and weather act as hot water on freeze dried crystals being poured over your innards. Delicious smells, like that of fresh coffee or, better, mountain laurel in the Spring, waft through you. Powers you didn't dream you had are drawn forth by your contact with The Wild Heart. These very powers are essential ingredients to address the current crisis in the human journey.

Your mentor now invites you to step into the center of the circle. The foundation of your previous work provides you with firm footing as you take your step. In the center of the circle, you are with your essence, your soul. You are at your still point. You are in the eye of the storm. You have navigated the intense storms in the bands surrounding the inner hurricane. At last you dwell at the edge of your true identity. The journey has brought you, for the moment, to your true self, or at the very least a portal to your true identity.

> *"I went to the woods because I wished to live deliberately, to front only the essential facts of life, and see if I could not learn what it had to teach, and not, when I came to die, discover that I had not lived."*
>
> Henry David Thoreau, *Walden*

You breathe. Soon, thoughts cease. Energy flows up through your bare feet, moving with your breath through tight spots in your body. The contractions slowly release. Your chest opens. Your shoulder blades slide down your back ever so slightly. Your heart has room for the fire of the Untamed to radiate through your arms and out your fingers. The call of a raven moving over the circle gently caresses you. A fresh breeze wraps its arms around you. The Sun feels warm on your skin.

> *"In such mystical moments you experience an Ever Present Origin. You have a primal trust as you know first hand 'the vegetative intertwining of all living things.'"*
>
> Jean Gebser, *The Ever Present Origin*

You rest in the simple feeling of Being. You are who you were before there was a planet Earth. You float in your Original Self.

10

The Witness Presence

After a long while, maybe an eternity, your mentor invites you out of the spiral. She has set up a stepladder and assists you in climbing safely up so you can look down at the spiral. Your mentor speaks softly summarizing your experience without adding or subtracting, acting as a mirror of the process. She repeats what she heard from your angry self voice, then the voice of fearful self. Next she focuses on the shadow selves with attention to the voice of inner patriarch and beyond to the golden self of hope and possibility. Your mentor then speaks with clarity, repeating what she heard from the Nature-based self, noting the freedom of the primordial energy in both the howling and the still point. Finally, she speaks softly of the soul/essence at the center of the spiral.

She asks you if you have any elaborations or corrections to her perceptions of your work. You look down from your perch on the ladder at these sub-selves, these sub-divisions of your inner council. You behold the pattern of this complex configuration without judgment or criticism. You simply witness. You are objective. You are neutral. You are not attached to outcome. Nor, do you move quickly to solutions to your individual problems or to the planetary crisis. In this state of consciousness, you are both entirely free and, at the same time, totally able to absorb what the different selves have expressed.

> You experience a freedom like none other.
>
> You don't have to decide anything.
>
> You don't have to engage in any practice.
>
> You don't have to go anywhere.
>
> You don't have to be anything.
>
> You have no identity in this state.
>
> You have no investment in outcome.
>
> You are free.
>
> You look at your compulsions and your addictions, but, for the moment, they don't have a hold on you.
>
> You are not even your essence or your soul, the essential you.
>
> You see your soul/essence, wonderful as you appear in the eye of the storm. But you are not even that. Anything you can see, you are not. Anything in the spiral beneath you is not all there is to you, because you are witnessing it. You are The Witness, pure and simple.

Gently, your mentor invites you to come down from your perch on the ladder. Her voice is a long way off in the distance. Slowly, you descend from the high place. Jesus ascended to the Mount of Transfiguration but then climbed down to engage the world. Buddha sat under a tree but got up to return and teach. You climbed a ladder. To enter the Sacred Council you must come down from the high place, as did they.

> *"... you are developing a capacity for strong meditative equanimity, a capacity to Witness both pain and pleasure without flinching, without either grasping or avoiding."*
> Ken Wilber,
> *One Taste*, p. 59

As you reach the solid ground once again, you laugh, and say to your mentor, "All of this from climbing on a ladder."

When we usher our shadow selves into the interior Sacred Council by way of the Witnessing Presence, we might think all would be well. Usually, this is not the case. Often an argument erupts between the newer selves and the operating ego selves. To that ongoing tension in the human saga we now move.

Robert Kegan, evolutionary psychologist, made this important discovery: as we develop we move to different levels of maturity and identity. We have an identity as a 5 year-old. Then, we grow to an 11 year-old and look back at who we were as a 5 year-old. Then, at age 18, we look back at who we were at 11. At age 40, we achieve a very different identity and look back at the 18 year-old. Then, Kegan makes this point: the subject at one level becomes the object at the next level. By that he means when we are 18, we are a subject and think that is really all there is to us. Then, at age 40, we achieve another level and the 18 year-old become the object of our witnessing. So, the subject becomes the object of our witnessing at each ensuing level of human evolution, ad infinitum.

The Evolving Self, 1982

11

Opposites in the Sacred Council

In the autumn of 1962, students at Emory University in Atlanta, Georgia, poured out of the buildings housing the various graduate schools. The structures faced inward on a quadrangle, and the grassy area held a variety of scholars making speeches and entering dialogue with the students. The scene was patterned after the free speech in Hyde Park in London. As a young man from far West Texas, I was new to this cosmopolitan atmosphere and wandered around with stars in my eyes. People from the Deep South sounded funny to me, and I, to them with my West Texas twang.

Near a stately Loblolly Pine tree, a black man spoke with inspiration and intelligence. I found myself captivated by his ideas and presence. At this stage of my life, I had never talked to a minority with a PhD. Such was the limitation of my provincial education. He advocated a philosophy of non-violence, a word new to me. He mentioned Borden Parker Bowne's philosophy, personalism, an area of my philosophical interest. He riveted my attention.

Students interacted with him, along with several of his supporters who followed him there. From one of his colleagues, I discovered the man was Martin Luther King, Jr., a name meaning little to me at the time. Within two years, he would win the Nobe

Peace Prize, and yet at this point he was not a household name, at least not in my West Texas neighborhood.

Answering my questions about where I might learn more from him, his supporters informed me Martin—as they called him—often preached in his father's congregation, Ebenezer Baptist Church. In fact, Martin and his father were co-pastors. Back in my tiny apartment, I couldn't get his expansive energy and ideas out of my system.

Some weeks later, I was assigned to Grady General Hospital in Atlanta for a clinical residency focused on counseling with persons traumatized with terminal illness. The hospital—segregated at the time—was located not too far from Ebenezer Baptist Church. I was assigned the cancer ward treating African American women. At age twenty-two, I was a Texas racial hybrid, and clueless. The women were patient and mainly counseled me. To my youthful chagrin vulnerability concerning illness and death floated into almost every conversation I had with the patients. I was at a loss as to how to be helpful.

Before long I found myself attending services at Dr. King's church to hear more of his teachings and find a cultural context for my clinical work at the hospital. The years rolled by, and I participated in civil rights marches, did menial work in the movement, and protested the Viet Nam war. In short, I came to know the elevated side of this remarkable man, known to us as Dr. King. Although he didn't know me personally, I felt I knew him well. Martin Luther King, Jr. became a hero and role model.

Later, I encountered disturbing information. While on marches, I heard rumors of another side of Dr. King, ones concerning his sexual conduct outside his marriage. At the time I dismissed the rumors because I couldn't hold in my mind and heart the opposites of the spiritual giant and the unfaithful husband. Decades passed.

In 1989, Ralph Abernathy wrote an autobiography, *And the Walls Came Tumbling Down*. I deeply respected Ralph Abernathy from my distant contact with him in the movement. He seemed a person of objectivity and integrity, so I wanted to see how he perceived himself and Dr. King. By that time I had struggled with bringing the spiritual selves and the sexual selves into Sacred Council within myself, and I was more open to Abernathy's perception of King's human struggle with opposites.

He wrote, "Martin and I were away more often than we were at home; and while this was no excuse for extramarital relations it was a reason. Some men are better able to bear such deprivations than others, though all of us in SCLC headquarters had our weak moments. We all understood and believed in the prohibition against sex outside of marriage. It was just that he had a particularly difficult time with that temptation."[1]

In my twenties I could not conceive of the elevated spiritual sub-self and the sexually unfaithful self being together in my hero. However, in my middle years, I had come to embrace the opposites in myself a bit more clearly and concluded that these pairs of opposites are part and parcel of the human condition.

> *"Everything that we see is a shadow cast by that which we do not see."*
>
> Martin Luther King, Jr

Seeing the Opposites

As we develop a witness consciousness, we build muscles of objectivity and neutrality. That is, we develop the capacity to see with clear eyes what is—without judgment, at least in our better moments. First, we see these opposites in people we love, hate, or both.

With clear and neutral eyes, we see not only Buddha's brilliant spiritual selves but also the opposite selves who could abandon his son for six years in the service of his adult journey to find himself.

We see Jesus' sub-self teaching that the meek will inherit the Earth and exhorting us to turn the other cheek. In stark contrast, another Jesus sub-self lashes out at the money changers in the Temple. Does he not practice what he teaches, or is he just struggling with opposites like the rest of us?

We see a non-violent Gandhi as a spiritual guru and social activist who changed the course of the world. When we delve deeper, we behold an opposite self who railed in anger at his wife and children.

We see Henry David Thoreau meditating in the wilderness, only to find that Walden Pond was a short distance from his mother's home where he often visited, during his two year vision quest (pause for effect) to do his laundry.

On a popular/political level we see Roosevelt, Eisenhower, Kennedy, Johnson, and Bill Clinton not only having brilliant leadership selves but also selves lacking in personal integrity in their marriages.

We see Hilary Clinton's having the toughness of a global warrior on the one hand and the vulnerable selves apparent in the New Hampshire primary on the other.

We see Tiger Woods as arguably the world's premier athlete and an impressive philanthropist showing humane selves in his sensitive work with inner city children, and then his opposite and insensitive selves breaking forth in extra-marital affairs.

> *"Black Elk (1863–1950) may well be the most famous Native American shaman, a visionary and medicine man."*
>
> Professor Dennis Hamm, (Creighton.edu)
>
> *"Black Elk was responsible for the conversion of 400 Natives to the Catholic Church."*
>
> Lucy Black Elk, Black Elk's daughter

We see Black Elk as the visionary whose teachings guided a generation into indigenous spirituality. Then we behold—to our great surprise—his opposite selves who led him in his middle years to teach traditional dogma for the Catholic Church as a catechist.

If we turn the eyes of this witnessing presence inward, as in the ecodrama in the preceding chapter, we will also see these public people are reflections of our own struggle to hold opposites in Sacred Council.

Holding Opposites in Sacred Council

From the vantage place of the ladder (and hopefully the vision mountain) with witnessing eyes, the mentee in the ecodrama saw her opposites. She saw her warrior selves angry with men and the opposites in her vulnerable selves. She saw the primitive howling of her primordial, nature-based selves and their opposites in the form of her consumer selves living in extravagance on the income of her spouse. In so doing, she held the opposites in the container of her visionary circle. As she held these opposites, she entered Sacred Council with her many selves.

Psychological maps of our inner world point to this ability to hold opposites as a mark of maturity. To hold them means to cease projecting our unresolved conflict with our inner opposites onto figures around us, both public and private. It means bringing into awareness the multitude of opposites dwelling within. It means exploring our shadow world and the tension between them and our primary selves to awareness.

> *"In formal logic, a contradiction is the signal of defeat, but in the evolution of real knowledge it marks the first step in progress."*
> Alfred North Whitehead

The Sweat of Opposites

Hal and Sidra Stone are the most important researchers and teachers I know of on the planet regarding the subject of our many inner voices; they offer brilliant maps through the terrain of the many selves. (The Indian philosopher and mystic, Aurobindo, is a close second.)

Once, several years ago, Judith Yost, my colleague and spouse, and I picked up Hal and Sidra up at their hotel for an evening of fun. Hal and Sidra had completed a day of intense teaching, during which they regaled students with their stunning approach to the human condition. As we drove to the restaurant, Hal spoke with the voice of a clown, making faces and doing impersonations leaving us in stitches of laughter. Who was he? The master teacher? The clown? Both?

Over our meal we talked about the tension between the expert psychologist and the clown. Our conversation moved to more difficult tensions between the opposites. Both Hal and I described the back and forth motion within the inner council as producing a physical sweat. I likened it to the ceremonial sweat lodge, one where the intense heat brings forth the opposites. I pointed to the ceremonial sweat lodge as being a key factor in both the inner Sacred Council of the Iroquois elders and the outer manifestation in their participatory democracy.

Sidra and Judith chose other metaphors, childbirth being one. The pain of standing between the opposites is akin to the birthing pains a woman feels. In the birth process many women report the powerful tension between the euphoria of motherhood and the pain and vulnerability of their body. Nature begins life with overwhelming tension, the birth trauma. The mother sweats. The child drips afterbirth. The child reclines on the mother's breast in mutual euphoria.

The Seesaw of Opposites

Often with my students I picture them on a playground seesaw. On one side of the seesaw is the primary self. On the other side of the seesaw is the shadow self, dangling legs in frustration. Eventually the shadow self gains enough weight through life conditions to throw the operating ego selves up in the air. The up and down motion goes back and forth,until sweat appears. After the work we explored in the ecodrama, the narrative recorded in the previous chapter, another presence appears on the seesaw from the ladder near-by. This presence stands on the seesaw and balances. It draws from both sides, encompassing the neutrality it gained from the witnessing presence. It becomes the *aware ego*.

12

The Amazing Aware-Go

Twenty students from Wisdom University sit on a deck in Santa Fe, New Mexico. Judith and I are teaching. We have discovered in our work with this unique organization that the seminar circle itself is a projection of our joint inner Sacred Councils. The initial teaching for us consists of listening to our many interior voices.

As faculty we provide a beginning map and a flexible structure, but we know our maps are not the territory of the learning terrain. What we think might happen is very different from the actual occurrence. We know the Sacred Council of students will teach us what to teach. We know a collaboration of creativity will blur the boundaries between students and faculty; *the Sacred Councils of students and faculty in tandem, become the teacher.* The model of leadership and learning for this day and time is not the guru teacher but the community itself.

On the deck overlooking a spring fed lake surrounded by towering cotton wood trees, we discuss the subject of this chapter, the theme of the sweat of

> **The wisdom circle of learning begins with developing an inner council of selves—a symphony of collaboration, co-operation, and creation. The inner council of the teacher is projected onto the class, for good or ill.**

opposites and the seesaw metaphor. In a moment of exuberance I shout out, "It's the aware-go balancing in the middle of the seesaw." I meant to say the aware ego, but aware-go popped out.

A brief silence ensues, and then rolls of laughter. The learning circle pokes a bit of fun by shouting, "The AWARE-GO." Then, it becomes a chant. Embarrassed at first, I soon see the genius of the council in the invention and embracing of a new word.

So, what is the aware-go?

Not a Thing, But a State

The aware-go is not a thing, a noun. It is a verb, or better, a moment in motion. It is a passing aspect of a state of consciousness we achieve from time-to-time. Often, the aware-go (aware ego) state arises after work on yourself, much like the work described in the preceding chapters. Sometimes, the aware-go is a gift of Nature. You wake up one morning with clear eyes and a pure heart. You see both sides of yourself in a given situation. You know this inner state is passing, but you offer gratitude and experience joy for the gift, savoring the moment.

The Aware-Go as Actual Occasion

Alfred North Whitehead, noted mathematician and philosopher, describes reality as a process punctuated by what he called actual occasions. Anyone who has studied Whitehead knows you never quite comprehend the nuances of his philosophical terms. In my cosmic map I use the term, actual occasion, to describe the experience of taking awareness from the high place and connecting it to the moment of clear choice and eventual practice; namely, the aware-go.[1] The aware-go is a fountainhead of actual occasions, the process of reality in motion.

States Into Traits

True: the aware-go only shows up from time to time. Still, as your practice of meditation, physical wellness, and psychological exploration continues, the state of mind called the aware-go arises more frequently, sometimes, even consistently.

As this evolution occurs, the aware-go appears frequently enough that others see this state as a trait of your character. If they mention such to you, it may puzzle you. You know much of your life is still lived being dominated by one set of selves or another. Yet, the balance is present enough for you to create an aware zone around yourself. This sometimes state of the aware-go can become a trait of character, a center of gravity on the spiral of your evolution.

The Aware-Go and Spaciousness

How do you know you are in the presence of a person energized by the aware-go state? You are surrounded by a spaciousness inviting you to be yourself. You have psychic elbow room. One student described it like this: "I feel like I have enormous permission to explore my many voices." Another student calls her mentor, "Dr. EP, short for Dr. Enormous Permission." The reference here is to spaciousness.

Further, you know you are in the aware-go when you allow many voices to sit down in your inner council. You find yourself being curious about the most outrageous images, voices, and feelings, arising and seeking expression. A sense of relaxation comes over you. Energy flows freely through you. Laughter erupts freely and easily. Like a high-performing athlete, you can move into action but with smooth and relaxed competence. You can pick up the bat, fishing gear, golf club, or tennis racquet with the paradox of a firm yet freely relaxed grip. Your sacred activism becomes natural, not forced. Your mentees feel challenged but respected. People feel pushed and challenged by your presence, yet strangely comforted by a sense of timelessness in your countenance. They sense in you the *Unqualifiable Mystery* balanced by the Earthiness of your Wild Heart.

Aware-Go Choices

Through balancing the back and forth of the inner seesaw, you gain perspective. Your choices take into account different points-of-view. Sometimes, you are a conservative Republican, who states that global warming is mainly within the purview of natural cycles, like solar activity. Sometimes, you are a liberal Democrat and argue strongly on behalf of the human role in the climate crisis as being the tipping point propelling us over the cliff into catastrophe. Often, you rise above the inner Democrat and the inner Republican and find an integral way. The Witness Presence lifts you toward a completely different political perspective, one the sociologist, Paul Ray, calls *the political north.*[2]

You balance between the opposites. You sweat. You witness from the high place. You transcend the opposites and include both perspectives. You return with the awareness of your witnessing vision of your opposites. Your choices gain the wisdom of both sides of yourself in a given situation. Because you stand in the balancing place and draw on either side, you are able to mentor people on both the left and right. You can contribute to choices and solutions drawing on the strength of both points-of-view.

> *"All perspectives have an element of truth, and no perspective has all of the truth. No one is totally right, or totally wrong."*
> Ken Wilber

Aware-Go Practices

Since your aware-go moments produce more balanced choices, you can support the choices with daily practices. Let's say the question of eating comes up through a symptom in your health. You have been listening to a cluster of selves sitting on the extreme side of the seesaw, ones who like to be a bad boys or girls and eat only what is pleasurable at the moment—food laced with sugar, salt, chemicals, and fat. You also listen to the opposite side of you, one who likes to be healthy and eat foods good for you and for the Earth. Each side of the opposite works some of the time in practice, but each dominates the ego space by thinking it works all of the time. Each sub-self has developed in response to a life condition and works for that condition.

However, new life conditions arise each day demanding a more complex approach. When these complex conditions arise, then the opposite side of the seesaw calls to you, saying, "Listen to me. I have the answer." It probably does have an answer but for a very specific condition. For example, eating a sweet may comfort your anxiety but not give you enduring energy for the larger task.

Let's say the challenge at hand is a conflict you have with someone you love. This task requires more than comfort food; it demands an integration of the two opposites. The integral practice takes the best of both approaches and leaves behind the worst. The technical term is transcend and include.

Continuing with the eating proposition, you have slightly elevated blood pressure. One side tells you to eat heart healthy food. The other side tells you to comfort yourself with whatever tickles your fancy. An aware-go practice might include the opposites by finding heart healthy food, which over time, comes to tickle your fancy. Sometimes, you hit the jackpot—the opposites can agree on eating chocolate.

Our culture is going through a similar situation with regard to petroleum-based autos. One side tells us to defend and protect our love of automobiles and the life style they afford. The other side tells us to move on to the alternative energy sources and to jettison the petro-chemical industry. The aware-go listens carefully to both sides. She affirms the genius of our many inventions running on fossil fuel and, at the same time, recognizes change has to emerge if we are to avoid a major collapse. She affirms the alternatives as they arise out of creative consciousness. She bends the opposites together in creative life styles. She builds homes around the planet running on alternative fuels. She drives autos running on electricity gathered from roofs and solar panels. If you open to it, you can see aware-go practices flowering in our midst.

The Aware-Go Is Essential to the Sacred Council

As we evolve inwardly, we eventually go through a process whereby our operating ego unfolds into the aware-go. The question of what makes the council sacred is now on the table with a direct statement.

The inner Sacred Council is essential for the larger Sacred Council in the form of alternative wisdom circles springing up around the planet. As you become more intimate with your interior gathering of selves, then you automatically are drawn to more profound intimate circles. As Sacred Councils manifest what I call Sacred Circles they become key players in working with the extreme events confronting us in the climate crisis. In this way we can see our inner work will absolutely determine the future of the human species.

> **The aware-go is a crucial element in our Sacred Inner Council. At the higher levels no council is sacred without a developed aware-go.**

Nature-Based (Indigenous) Selves Are Key Players for Current Sacred Councils

In order to have an inner Sacred Council fully addressing current issues, we need an aware-go, one fully informed by Nature-based selves. If we are to confront Earth's current crisis, we will have to bring into our inner council Earth-based selves. It's as simple as that. They wait in the wings. They are our culture's shadows. They have been pushed out of our awareness and practice for a hundred years. Many learning circles cultivate the aware-go, yet a firm connection with the Web of Life in Nature is not there. Nature-based experiences in the wild are inconvenient even to those who adhere to inconvenient truths about the environment. (Are you listening, Al Gore?)

Solutions to the environmental crisis without the Wild Heart selves is a bit like a group of white folks going to the inner city to solve minority problems. A person of color comes forward and says, "You can't do anything to solve our community's problems unless you include us in the conversation." Similarly, when it comes to environmental issues, you can't do anything until you include the untamed voices from the loins of Mother Earth. The solutions lie in the Primordial Mind.

Some people currently functioning at a high level of the aware-go often do not have this crucial member present and active within the inner council. Even among cultural creatives and environmental activists, this absence of mystical connection with Nature becomes evident when we scratch the liberal surface.

Where are John Muir, Walt Whitman, and Henry David Thoreau when we need them most?

Perhaps, they hide in Ken Wilber's considerable works. In Wilber's Cosmic Map, Nature Mysticism shows up as the foundation of his study of the human pilgrimage. In Wilber's schemes you occasionally get the full force of his Natural Mystic connection, though it is often obscured with a stunning variety of intellectual systems. You especially feel the throb of the Wild Heart connection in his wife Treya as she navigates illness and approaching death.

The moving account of the Wilbers shared voyage through the trauma of her cancer and eventual death reveals her as a courageous Natural Mystic; she is full of *Grace and Grit*, the title he gives to the narrative. Time and again she reaches up to pull Ken out of the clouds of his philosophical systems and complex meditations to ground him in the simple being of hearing rain on the roof.

As death approached Treya, gale-force winds buffeted their home. Ken wrote: "The best, the strongest, the most enlightened, the most honest, the most beautiful, the most inspiring, the most virtuous, the most cherished person I had ever known, had just died. Somehow, I felt that the universe would never be the same."[3]

Where would he turn? How could he possibly navigate this turbulence? A close friend touched him on the shoulder, saying, "Listen. Listen to that." The gale force winds had completely ceased blowing, and the Universe, their Universe, was perfectly calm. It wasn't the same; it was calmer.

Ken later wrote: "This (the ceasing of the winds), too, was dutifully noted in the next day's papers, right to the exact minute. The ancients have a saying: 'When a great soul dies, the winds go wild.' The greater the soul, the greater the wind necessary to carry it away."[4]

Some observers refer to Wilber as the quintessential thinker of the 21st Century, and that may well be so. The roots of his work keep returning to the simple but profound connection with the numinous of Nature.

That said, let's look briefly at Wilber's model of the evolution of the mystical connection in humans with the Greater Whole in order to grasp the importance of the foundation for our journey.[5]

- The first mystics in the human story were Nature Mystics. They practiced their spiritual connections in the forests, mountains, and deserts. The Iroquois Council is a good example, as is a young Black Elk.

- Next the Deity Mystics come into view. These are the Judaeo/Christian/Islamic monotheists who emphasize spiritual oneness with Deity, the Great Other. Rumi, C.S. Lewis, and St. Francis are examples. A middle-aged Black Elk is also an example of the Deity Mystic. The focus here moves away from experience of the Mystery in Nature to scripture about God. The seeker uses Nature and scripture to experience deeply the Otherness of God.

- Next in the evolution of spirituality, Unity mystics teach students to become One with the One as in Hindu mysticism. Muktananda is an example. A basic suspicion of being attached to the natural order is seen in this approach. The seeker pushes the Nature-based self into the shadows as a distraction from mystical union.

- Finally, emerges the non-dual mystic who integrates essential elements from all of the above. The Dalai Lama is an example. Black Elk achieved this form of consciousness in his elder years.

Throughout Wilber's lengthy works you behold how humans began their spiritual journey with The Great Tree, the Sacred Wind, the night sky, and all living creatures. Such powerful connections in Nature lie at the heart of the primordial human voyage. In order to face the complexity of evolving life conditions, their spirituality became more ornate as time passed, and the migrations filled the Earth with humans. To make a very long story short, today humans have lost the power of that root energy. In calling for a return of the Wild Heart, I am not suggesting we do only that. I suggest we follow the lead of the Dalai Lama and the later Black Elk and return to our roots without losing the brilliance of later developments.

As we transcend, we will have to descend to that structure of consciousness where the Wild Heart lives, so we can include her to balance out modern and post-modern civilization.

The importance of descending the spiral of evolution from the immense complexity of our evolving culture to ancient wisdom as basic building blocks cannot be overstated. Look at the following analogy to grapple with this point.

As we evolve scientifically and medically, we discover the reality of cell communication within our bodies. Health, it seems, depends on how our cells communicate with each other. The organism of the person depends on the heart. The heart depends on the cells. The cell depends on the molecules. The molecule depends on the sub-atomic particles, which form the foundation of the material world, including our bodies. These particles reaching back to the first milliseconds of the Big Bang are units of energy. They move throughout our bodies, exchanging information about our inner council, and interfacing with environmental influences.

Physical health depends on the ability of the person to move *down the spiral of evolution* to the foundation of the person, the cell, the sub-atomic particle, or even these discrete units of energy bouncing around inside called quantum waves. Without the cell the heart can't function,nor the kidney, nor the lungs.

So it is with non-dual or integral mysticism, which depends on unity mysticism, which depends on deity mysticism, which then depends on Nature mysticism. Without Nature-based mysticism, non-dual mysticism cannot function, especially in relation to the complex problems of the environmental crisis.

The Nature-based self is to the Sacred Inner Council what the cell is to the body. It is the basic building material for the vessel of the aware-go as it carries us through the white water of crisis.

Put another way, the aware-go must descend the spiral of evolution through the various levels of human development to retrieve the Nature-connection

With these comments as a context, review our current situation. If the Indigenous or Wild Hearted self sits in the cultural creative council at all, she does not have a deciding vote. You can see this lack in the Reagan, Clinton, two Bushes, and Obama administrations. Many good people with sometimes high functioning aware-gos work in these administrations. Bill Clinton, for example, quotes Ken Wilber. Clinton is a sometimes integral thinker, but I do not receive the impression of a sub-self in his inner council deeply influenced by Nature. President Obama tips his talented hat at the environmental crisis, yet little sense of a personal and deep connection with Nature comes through thus far in his administration.

Contrast these administrations with Teddy Roosevelt. While flawed in many ways, Roosevelt had a profound, first-hand, Nature-based connection that made up for many shortcomings. Without Teddy we would have very few National Parks, these pockets of the wild calling to the inner core of humanity.

Ken Burns, the groundbreaking video artist, calls our National Parks, America's Best Idea. I underlined this point earlier, and it too cannot be overstated. Why? Early Nature visionaries saw the Wild Heart of the Americas as crucial. At the risk of being naïve and simplistic, I suggest the building blocks to addressing our current crisis lie in learning the basics of making campfires, setting up tents, tending gardens, sharing wilderness hikes, eating camp food and wild berries. Such practices allow us to lie alone in the wilderness with the night sky, to vision quest, to contact the invisible forms available in all the biosphere, and to live with dangers and possibilities bigger than preserving our addictive life styles at all costs.

> **On a 1 to 1000 scale our cultures live with the illusion we can control Nature at about a 700 level. As we live closer to Nature, we discover this bit of wisdom: our control is about .0001.**

13

The Sacred Council in Action

Paradoxically, as we discover the limits of our control through living closer to the rhythms of nature, we encounter solutions. As Nature teaches us to let go of one kind of safety and control, we gain another. Every downhill skier knows what I mean. As you ski downhill, your common sense control tells you to lean back when you hit a bump. If you follow common sense control and lean back, you fall. If, on the other hand, you lean out over your skis and boots—counter to what your ordinary protection and control system tells you—you discover another form of control. Leaning down hill, strangely, opens up more possibility of fun, beauty, and safety. Let's see what I mean by this paradox.

Earlier I underscored the poverty of our contemporary national leaders in this regard. Regardless of party affiliation, American leaders continue to rely on the hubris of dominance as a way to seek safety. The U.S. now spends more on defense (translates as command and control) than the rest of the world combined. Other world leaders have faired better.

A defining event from Gandhi's life comes to mind. At a critical stage in the liberation of India from Great Britain, the British placed a tax on salt in an attempt to tighten the screws of control on the nonviolent campaign for freedom rumbling across India's countryside. They reasoned they would put these *colored* folks in their place. Who were these *colored* upstarts to challenge the most powerful (at that time) empire in the world?[1]

Prominent politicians in the Indian liberation movement came to Gandhi asking for his leadership in confronting the *evil* Empire. Was it an *evil* empire? Any organization of humans addicted to control and domination becomes darker and darker until *evil* is an apt description. Certainly, the people of India experienced their repression as evil, even as American colonists knew the evil of taxation without representation levied on them by the same British.

Gandhi did not respond to the requests of the young firebrands immediately. Much to their dismay, he retreated into meditation in his garden, a beautiful place with stately trees, lush foliage, and brilliant flowers. The critical situation of the salt tax demanded actions and answers, but first he sought the still point within his own inner council. Perhaps, he desired to lean into the complex questions.

From the edge of the garden, the smells and sounds of the nearby River Sabarmati renewed the spirits of the liberators, discouraged as they were. Did Gandhi hope an interior sub-self—some hidden resource—would be called forth through not only his meditation but through the contact with birds and flowers from the lush garden?

> *The Mahatma loved being close to Nature in this setting. He once said, "This is the right place for our activities to carry on the search for truth and develop fearlessness, for on one side are the iron bolts of the foreigners, and on the other the thunderbolts of Mother Nature."*
>
> Gandhi,
> wiki/SabarmatiAshram

A few days passed. The young Indian leaders grew evermore restless and pressed Gandhi for a strategy. Still, he meditated. More time. More pressure. The meditation continued. The younger followers doubted their diminutive mentor with round glasses on his mid-nose, and murmured among themselves. Was he behind the times? Was he out-of-touch with stark reality in his cheery hopefulness? Was he too spiritual for these tough political questions?

Still unclear, Gandhi had an inner sense that he must walk. His meditations were incomplete in his protected space. He spoke of listening to an inner voice. But which inner voice? He wrote later of many voices within, so it seems he was searching for some voice not available in the comforts of his own living quarters, even if it included a garden.

It seems simple when spiritual advisers tell us to listen to our inner voice, but Gandhi didn't know which voice was spiritual. Hinduism offers a plethora of spiritual voices, and Gandhi did not limit himself to Hinduism. So, even if he found a spiritual voice, which spiritual voice's guidance was right for this moment?

And so, he walked out of his garden past the hopeful followers. They questioned him once again; but, much to their continued disappointment and consternation, he did not answer. He walked through the suburbs of the city of Ahmadabad, along its river banks. Frustrated, his fellow liberators walked with him, not knowing what they were doing or what else to do. As he ambled along light-heartedly, stick in hand, he sensed a pull of the ocean to the West. He was a child of Western India, and so the haunts of his childhood ecology beckoned to him. His senses were alive, and his allies from the natural order reached out to him, offering guidance.

> It is no accident that Grandmother Nature pulled Gandhi and his followers West, literally West. In ancient wisdom traditions, West is the direction of hidden truth, of shadows, of the dying of old habits and patterns, and of the setting Sun.

Newspaper images of that march show his fellow freedom workers with drums and other instruments, often barefooted. Marchers joined and then faded, but a core of seventy-eight die-hards stayed with him, all the while not knowing what they were doing or where they were going.

For a little over three weeks—23 days to be exact—these freedom seekers moved through a natural world of challenging terrain, seeking a way through their national crisis, hopefully a way not involving military action and violence. Along the march one of the truth-seekers, Paluskar, sang Gandhi's favorite spiritual songs. They must have been quite a sight on their Nature hike, singing, chanting, drumming, and yet barely talking. Villagers noticed their sore and bleeding feet and threw water on the hard roads to soften the way. In places along the path the chanting supporters placed flowers and fresh vegetation to offer a cushion.

After 237 miles of their Nature pilgrimage, they could smell the Sea of Arabia. They did not speak much, but rather had an intuitive rapport bordering on the telepathic—a gift of their walking quest. Still, the Mahatma had not disclosed his intent. Most likely, the social action strategy was still fermenting as he continued to draw on the deep ecological base as he ambled along. Later, Gandhi would write about what made his action, Sacred Activism. First and foremost he fasted to clarify his profound connection to Nature, a point many scholars overlook.

> *"I need no inspiration other than Nature's. She has never failed me yet. She mystifies me, bewilders me, sends me into ecstasies. Beside God's handiwork does not man fade into insignificance?"*
> Gandhi

On April 5, 1930, Gandhi and his truth-seekers reached the coast near the sleepy village of Dandi. They gathered on the beach, offering prayers to the West, prayers to the waters, and prayers to all living things, culminating in Hindu chants of devotion. The Mahatma spoke simply and briefly. At long last his strategy became clear. He picked up a tiny lump of salt mixed with beach sand. The British watched, and an empire held its breath. Yet, he had not broken the law just by picking up the sand.

He built a fire. (Now, we have crucial elements of a revolution: earth, air, fire and water.) He boiled the seawater and made the commodity forbidden by British law—salt. Within moments the force of the truth of his civil disobedience spread like the fire boiling the water, until the marchers and the countryside supporters were aflame. Everywhere people picked up salt and joined in a massive demonstration of non-violent action. Fires dotted the beach for miles, as the now budding revolutionaries joined joyfully in the free gift of the sea—salt.

Henry David Thoreau must have leaped with joy to see his principles spring into action. Thoreau wrote in *Civil Disobedience*: "The law will never make a man free; it is men who have got to make the law free." That Gandhi was inspired by Thoreau, the quintessential person of Nature, is clear. Look at some of Gandhi's inspirational thoughts and see the beat of the primordial heart, far deeper than usual political activism:

> *"I believe in nature cures and fasting."*
>
> *"The Earth provides enough to satisfy every man's needs, but not every man's greed."*
>
> *"When I admire the wonders of a sunset or the beauty of the moon, my soul expands in the worship of the creator."*
> Gandhi[2]

If you want to know the quality of the internal environment of Sacred Councils needed for our day, then look at the fire of these two men—Gandhi and his inspiration, Thoreau

- Look at the inner selves gathered around the fire.
- Look at a Witnessing Presence giving them detachment from domination by first one self and then another.
- Look at the expanding awareness as they work on themselves.
- Look at the choices and the actions flowing out of these inner councils.
- Look at the basic starting place in the garden by the river or the cabin by the lake.

Above all notice that it took only seventy-eight people aflame with their Wild Hearts to turn the course of the world with the lighting of a single fire.

Let's look at another example of hope emerging through the power of humans to turn a corner toward a larger story. Be aware how the deep connection with Nature bursts forth out of hiding to surprise us.

The Apollo Program was a NASA spaceflight endeavor that landed the first humans on Earth's moon. It was a dream of one of our great Presidents, Dwight Eisenhower. On May 25, 1961, John Kennedy took the torch of Eisenhower's dream/vision with a state-of-the-union address calling for "landing a man on the Moon" by the end of the decade.[3] This goal was accomplished on July 20, 1969.

How?

The usual ego expanded through dreamtime to include in active consciousness a larger set of selves, including the scientific, the adventurer, and the intentional selves. Amidst the chaos of societal unrest in the 1960's many dreams emerged and came to fruition. As a nation we were mired in assassinations, war, and repression of civil rights. But we found inspiration in what many believed at the time was our greatest accomplishment—a person on the moon. In retrospect walking on the Moon may not have been the apex of our journey. Nature surprised us with something we had not expected.

The last Apollo flight in 1972 resulted in what some historians think is the most important accomplishment of the Apollo Space Program: a photo of the Earth from the perspective of outer space. That photo continues to shift consciousness. In it we see ourselves from a distance as never before in a stunning evocation of the Witnessing Presence, reaching across the span of humanity.

> If we hold a dream geared ultimately to the sustainability of our planet Earth, then the Earth dream nurtures and enhances life in ways we cannot imagine.

Eisenhower and Kennedy gave birth to a dream in the throws of a cold war fueled by competition in the space race and fraught with the raging fear of the Communist menace. Their dream had within it a deep seed of hope and beauty, an essence even they could not know. Scientists labored with technological goals, and they were worthy.

Yet, within their dream, secret hopes burst forth through a single photograph. The taking of the photograph was actually an afterthought of NASA planning, a throwaway comment in a larger conversation. The image of Earth showed her wild, blue beauty wrapped in swirls of clouds against the black of deep space. The Wild Heart of Earth reveals Herself in mysterious ways touching our consciousness and swelling our hearts in our chests when we least expect it.

"Is this who we are?" We ask ourselves as we look at Earth's image. We catch a glimpse. We catch our breath. We gulp. We contemplate.

Who would know that a once angry attorney in India would transform his inner council and show the modern world the wild freedom of non-violence? Who would know that a military hero morphed into a Republican President would plum his inner council and lead us in the direction of outer space and the Witnessing Presence? Who would know a simple photograph would impact our consciousness in ways that may dwarf the actual walking on the moon?

And where can we now turn today for a profound myth to plug us into the neural network of Earth's Wild Heart in the fashion of the first photograph of our planet from space?

14

Tails in the Avatar Tale

In the 1960's I read Carl Jung's *Memories, Dreams, and Reflections.* A powerful image was presented in the book, or so I thought. Jung depicts humans as having a hose extending from the bottom of the spine down into a substratum of human existence he calls the collective unconscious. At the base of the spine is a spigot to turn the hose on and off. Most dreams occur with the spigot turned off, so the dream is basically from the personal unconscious, not the collective. Such dreams assist the person but don't relate to the larger human story.

Sometimes, though, it becomes apparent to the dreamer and to the therapist that the spigot opens by the hidden hand of personal or environmental influences. Up from the collective unconscious flows a dream or a myth or a vision applying to all humanity, indeed all reality. These dream/visions are of enormous significance because they provide the potential to link with other bytes of information coming through other living creatures to form a pattern. These patterns offer the possibility of becoming intricate maps to guide the human pilgrimage. This connecting of the dots into a holistic pattern tells us, as anthropologist Gregory Bateson asserted in the title of his important book: *Mind and Nature (Are) A Necessary Unity.*[1]

My proposal suggests a primary way to turn the spigot to the open position is to journey out of civilized space into the wild as indicated in the Salt March narrative. As I write, it rains outside, a cold rain. I am warm and comfortable. A whole set of selves work through me as I write. If I open the door, feel water on my face, and walk a few paces in the rain, an entirely different complex of selves show up, including the wilder ones. I connect the dots of my civilized selves with my wilder, survival selves.

That wilder and freer self can turn the spigot to the open position to facilitate a larger story than my own. Such an untamed sub-self is not the only option for opening the spigot, but it is a crucial one we have all but lost in our daily lives, save unconscious hints that bubble through the spigot from time to time.

> *"In the wilderness is the preservation of the world."*
> Henry David Thoreau, *Walden*

The ravishing hunger for these undomesticated selves to hold a place in our culture can be seen in wild game hunters who unconsciously seek, in a sometimes twisted practice, the connection in the trophies on their walls. The hunger shows up in naming our autos mustangs, cougars, explorers, expeditions, tundras typhoons, scouts, trackers, mountaineers, navigators, foresters, freelanders , blazers, pathfinders, trailblazesr, and avalanches.

Why do we seek the riches of the collective unconscious through hunting expeditions and cars with such names? Unconsciously we hope wisdom will flow up from the depths through the hoses dangling from our spines and then circulate throughout our total beings. In this way Earth's story gets bigger and deeper, not smaller.

Award winning physicist, David Bohm, describes the depths as "the implicate order seeking to become explicate."[2] Jean Gebser argues for a retrieval of those qualities from the inner being that reach back to the archaic, the primordial mind, or that form of consciousness where there is "complete non-differentiation between man and the Universe."[3]

In preparation for the writing of this book, I dragged my tattered copy of Jung's book off a top shelf. I hadn't looked at it for some time, but I was certain I could find the reference. After awhile I found the page. To my surprise it wasn't Jung's metaphor of the spinal hose at all, but rather my image, one I created. Inspired by Jung's words, I had drawn in the margin a crude human stick figure with a hose dangling out of the tailbone. All these years I had been quoting Jung when, in fact, I had projected my image onto Jung's works. My apologies go to countless students throughout my psychotherapy and teaching career for misquoting Jung. Still, I love the image. It remains my waking dream.

In a similar vein you can recognize these archetypal images when they grab you and shake you with passion. Out of the vast collective unconscious, the implicate order, bubbles up the movie, *Avatar*. It shook many of us like a passion. James Cameron, the movie's creator, turned the spigot for both himself and now for the world-at-large.

Like *Star Wars* the movie, *Avatar*, doesn't make rational sense. Recently, I heard an interview with George Lucas as he reflected on the creative process in regards to *Star Wars*. He painted a picture for NPR where he took his script to the money people to see if he could secure financing. They read the script and pronounced indignantly, "It doesn't make sense. We don't get it."[4]

It doesn't make sense to the operating ego, only to the mythic selves sitting in the inner council of the aware-go. They are close friends with the Wild Heart. The same could be said for *Avatar*. Material from the vast field of information Jung called the collective unconscious does not make sense at a usual, rational level. Yet, these mythic movies have enormous appeal.

Within a month *Avatar* grossed over a billion dollars. Critics denounced the film as being superficial in the romanticizing of Nature. They pointed out Nature's chaos and disturbance of human endeavors through earthquakes, hurricanes, floods, and droughts. True enough. Still, Cameron tapped into hidden, if sometimes dark, depths. The mythic images are so powerful that more humans now have seen *Avatar* than any other film in entertainment history.

In Chapter 4, I described a group of people gathered around a fire on a cold, rainy day. I suggested they rolled out of bed and comfort because they were hungry for something, but what? Billions of dollars were spent around the world to see *Star Wars* and *Avatar*, because people know intuitively the profound solutions to our current dilemma lie in the images bubbling up through the hose in creative people. We humans are desperately hungry for the possibility inherent in the images and messages. As I indicated earlier, the advertising world well knows about our hunger.

Let's explore for a moment a few of these images in *Avatar*. Recall some of the basics of the plot. In 2154, in a distant star system, a corporation is mining Pandora, a lush, Earth-like, moon of the planet, Polyphemus. The Na'vi, a blue-skinned species of humanoids with feline characteristics, inhabit Pandora. Keep in mind, Jung thought cats suggested the divine feminine while dogs, the divine masculine. We will return to that point in a moment. Physically much stronger and taller than Earthly humans, the Na'vi live in harmony with Nature, worshiping a mother goddess called Eywa.

The Na'vi have two tails—a tail extending from their spine and a ponytail in the form of a hairstyle. Both are important images to the movie, but more so the pony tail. When the Na'vi need a deeper wisdom to face the unbridled greed of the invading corporation, they connect their ponytails with the roots of a significant tree. The tips of the ponytails sparkle with energy and a download occurs. Note the name of the first tree encountered in the movie—the Tree of Voices.

It seems the connection with the tree allows the many voices of the inner and outer world to speak to the Na'vi. This energy connection through the tendrils of their pony tails allows them to link with the consciousness of the animals, trees, and indeed the whole biosphere of their planet. They can hear the voices of their ancestors long gone and feel their own ancient spirits by plugging into the Tree of Voices. This process is not unlike the Ecodrama

I mentioned in Chapter 11 or like Voice Dialogue as practiced by Hal and Sidra Stone in *Embracing Ourselves*.

The corporation doesn't understand this strange bond. The wisdom embedded in the connection with the tree escapes them, and they bulldoze down the Tree of Voices. Not all is lost. It is also revealed that the planet Pandora has a network of trees which the Na'vi can tap into and receive unlimited, useful, and life-saving data, information, knowledge, and even wisdom. This network is something like a prodigious, planetary brain. The link to their ordinary reality and the trans/ordinary reality comes through their ponytail tendrils as neural links. The hair itself contains neural tentacles and features unknown to Earth humans.

The main character, Jake, is a Marine who has been sent there to assist the corporation. He has a double, an avatar, he can change into with the goal of infiltrating the natives of Pandora to enhance corporate profit. His avatar is a Na'vi, a physical form he changes into through transformative technology. In that form Jake appears in a blue body, ponytail and all.

> *"Recent neural research indicates neural cells extend out of the brain in the skull to the heart, the intestines, and perhaps elsewhere in the human body. This research gives credence to the folk wisdom of listening through your heart and gut reactions."*
>
> Bruce Lipton, Biologist, in *Spontaneous Evolution*

At one point, captured by a rival within the Na'vi, he is taken to the home tree. They are on to his corporate spying. In a threat most severe to the Na'vi, the rival warrior holds up his double-edged knife in a move to cut off Jake's ponytail. This metaphor harkens back to the Samson myth in tribal Judaism. Cutting off the *connection* is the most drastic punishment imagined by the Na'vi.

To them the ponytail is an extension of the spinal cord, a crucial connection to Grounded Wisdom. Modern humans might put the knife to the throat, center of expression. Not the Na'vi. To them the connection to the tree (in this case through the ponytail) is all important. Recall Jean Gebser's description of "the vegetative intertwining of all living things." (If such a connection seems too far-fetched, recall the name given by the Iroquois to the first signer of the Declaration of Independence, *The Great Tree*.)

Later in the movie the action moves to the Tree of Souls, the center of Na'vi spirituality and culture and even more important than the Tree of Voices. The corporation attempts to destroy the Tree of Souls but fails after a predictable conflict, punctuated with typical Hollywood excess in noise and visual violence. Again, the connection between the ponytails is seen as dipping into the Wisdom of the ages through the Tree of Souls. The ponytail is film creator's, James Cameron, version of the hose in my stick figure.

Questions come to mind concerning the image of trees and the role of Mother Nature in this mythical movie. With cynicism, modern and postmodern pundits point to what they call "the fury of Mother Nature," as in the recent earthquakes in Haiti and Chile. They rightly point out the folly of Nature-lovers who romantically want to live without the benefits of technology such as air conditioning, cell phones, autos, and the Internet. I say "rightly points out" in the sense there has never been an example in history where humans move as a mass to an earlier time in culture where there was less protection from the hardships sometimes imposed by the challenges of Nature.

Once humans crossed over the bridge from hunter/gatherers to horticulture and then agriculture, said cultures never returned to the former states. Once we humans crossed over the bridge from agriculture to the industrial age, we did not go back to the farm. Once we crossed over from the industrial to the informational, we did not return. At least so far, we have not made such a cultural downshift.

Let me clarify. Certainly, individuals and small groups descend the spiral of evolution to less complex life styles. Such descent is absolutely necessary. The movie/myth *Avatar* speaks to us strongly that we have left behind some gifts from each stage of human culture. If we are to survive as a species, we will need to descend to the

Primordial Mind to retrieve what has been lost. In earlier books I describe this descent as soul retrieval.

That said, I do not suggest we eliminate the benefits of our human advances, except when certain practices threaten to destroy us. My proposal seeks to balance the modern with the Primordial Mind and Wild Heart. The image of the Sacred Council with room for both the ancient, wild, and modern voices is crucial. On the one hand we have the naïve romantic voices in love with nature outings and, on the other hand, cynical voices cut off from any meaningful ties to Nature. These opposites both need a voice. In balance we will discover hope.

Recall *Avatar* ends with the unaware capitalists being banished from the planet. However, the Na'vi choose to keep the humans versed in the newer sciences as trusted and useful companions. At this point Cameron, the director of the film, suggests an integral approach, the balance of the wild and the modern.

Prominent in *Avatar* is the battle between the human corporation and the primal beings on that distant planet. It wouldn't be Hollywood without guns and violence. With the sound of gunfire in our ears, I move our discussion from the inner environment to the outer world with this question: "What is at the base of most human conflict?"

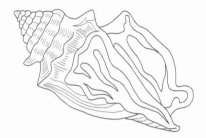

Sacred Council Bond

"I found one day in school a boy of medium size ill-treating a smaller boy. I expostulated, but he replied:'The bigs hit me, so I hit the babies; that's fair.' In these words he epitomized the history of the human race."

— Bertrand Russell,
   Education and the Social Order

"I am friends with thunder and lightning. Lightning hits close. It is my friend. It doesn't frighten me. But I don't do marriage counseling. Too dangerous."

— Rolling Thunder, Cherokee Shaman

"I would venture to warn against too great intimacy with artists as it is very seductive and a little dangerous."

— Queen Victoria (1819-1901)

15

Councils in Conflict

On the one hand, the human story consists of stunning beauty in the unfolding of awareness and compassion. On the other hand, our human tendency toward conflict is—to say the least—perplexing.

Questions arise: What is at the base of human conflict and violence? More personally, the question might be, "Why do I have so much conflict in my life, especially with those I love?" Then, a question appears that might be even more disturbing, "Why is it that I get along pretty well with people, yet don't really feel intimate with them?" Let's pursue the truths underneath these questions.

Earlier in this book I point to the built-in tension of opposites in the inner council of selves. Therein lie the seeds of our more or less constant conflict. To paraphrase an earlier musing from Gandhi, "Everywhere my many I's go, they go with me, and they tend to get upset with people around me." Why is that so? What purpose does Nature have in mind through habitual conflict in humans, not to mention our tendency to engage in war?

> "War is the worst environmental pollution. Yet, war comes from inner pollution."
> Rolling Thunder, Indigenous Shaman

Conservative groups espouse family values, but any police person will tell you that many dangerous calls involve intervention into family fights. The most perilous place to be on a Saturday night might be your own home.

If family dynamics create considerable conflict, perhaps you should turn to religion for assistance. Well, maybe. Judaism, Christianity, and Islam all advocate love, yet they have spawned the most dangerous era in our planet's history through conflict within and without. Lest Americans think I refer here to radical Islam alone, consider the violence of terrorist bomber, Timothy McVeigh, a strict Catholic and conservative Republican.

If cultural creative liberals think I refer only to conservatives, consider Greenpeace. Founder, Patrick Moore, calls his former comrades "a band of scientific illiterates who use Gestapo tactics."[1]

When we face squarely our current planetary crisis, the specter of terrorists gaining access to nuclear weapons has to be near the top of the list. In an interview with news analyst, Lou Dobbs, legendary American capitalist, Warren Buffett, said, "...thousands of years ago we had psychotics and we had religious fanatics, but about the most they could do was throw a stone at somebody... Right now there's the knowledge around to use nuclear material. And we've got to hope that the wrong people don't get their hands on it."[2] I could go on, but you get the idea.

What is the origin of all this violence?

War, it seems, begins with our internal wars, or as Rolling Thunder put it, *our inner pollution*. If that reality were not enough, consider this question. Why does Nature allow war and conflict anyhow? *Allow* may even be an understatement. *Encourage* the tension and conflict might be more apt.

> **We project the conflict of our inner council onto other people and groups so that our inner turmoil projects outward as relational, regional, and then planetary conflict. Our psycho/spiritual fight with ourselves becomes our fight with others, eventuating in global conflict.**

Preliminary answer to the above:

Conflict (including trauma and crisis) is Nature's way of drawing into our awareness zone (vision circle) the very sub-selves needing our attention.

Toward what end does this uncontrollable and sometimes chaotic aspect of Nature lead us? Another dimension of my proposal is this: only by paying close attention to these sub-selves brought forth in conflict can we expand our consciousness and move to the next level of evolution, individually and culturally.

In the concluding chapters of Part III I will show:

- Our inner councils bond with the inner councils of others.
- The bonding patterns often result in negativity.
- These negative bonding patterns lie at the base of all human conflict and thus global terror.
- Out of this conflict arises illimitable possibility.

Hal and Sidra Stone summarize our human condition succinctly in this way: "There are only three ways we know of that humans bond with each other.

- Positive bonding , which sweeps conflict under the rug in denial.
- Negative bonding, which inflames and dramatizes conflict.
- Intimacy, which works through conflict."[3]

Let's explore this bonding of our inner councils with other councils a bit further.

16

Fire in the Council

Imagine your inner council as a carefully laid fire in its potential stage. On the floor of the fire, next to the ground where the fire might start, are dry logs. These dry logs provide a foundation so the fire can spring up at a moment's notice. Additionally, sitting on top of the logs, you have a tipi of oily juniper cuttings dried by hot Sun; they extend above the logs to about waist high. Placed carefully around the tipi are two-inch diameter oak limbs, ready to burn. Mixed throughout is dried grass and thick combustible mulch. The Sun is warm, and a Southwest wind blows. All you need is ignition. Someone comes along, lights a match, and, boom, the fire roars.

In our inner council the ignition system—the match in this case—is always our *hidden vulnerability*. By hidden vulnerability I mean those sensitive sub-selves in our council easily hurt by the outside world. I say **hidden because we often push our tendency to be hurt to the rim of the council's circle**. Because of our sensitivity and vulnerability, we are walking-around, well-laid bonfires, waiting for the next match to ignite us.

As soon as the vulnerable selves feel hurt by the outside world, strong warriors in the inner council leap forward to attack the outside threat. On-the-ground action of the warriors is so swift that inner vulnerabilities are shunted off into the shadows before they have a chance to speak. What you feel and what the world sees is the force and often anger of the inner warriors. The warriors themselves usually are not aware they are fighting to protect the vulnerable. Their nature is to fight, not to be aware. Soon, they habituate to fighting for fighting's sake. Their weapons of choice are judgment, criticism, sarcasm, belittlement, arrogance, withdrawal, cruelty,and hard reasoning, to name a few.

Let's see how this dynamic works with the environmental crisis. At some level all of us feel a strong vibration of vulnerability because our planet is in crisis, and humans are at extreme risk. At an archaic level we all feel this humming danger either consciously or unconsciously.

In this general context, two friends talk.

They were college roommates and close friends. Their lives went in very different directions after graduation. One became an officer in a large petro-chemical corporation; the other, a psychologist and professor. They love each other as brothers, but they are bonfires waiting to happen when the subject of the climate crisis enters their conversation.

Corporate Man (CM): This climate crisis stuff is a total fabrication. I can't believe you would fall for Al Gore's political agenda in the form of scare tactics. I follow Michael Crichton's line of thinking in his novel, *State of Fear*.[1] He has a plot stating eco-terrorists attempt mass murder to support their views. Environmentalists capitalize on fear. You are fear mongers. We have enough fear without your embellishments. We all know your data is BS.

Professor Man (PM): The consensus of the world's scientists tells us that we are about to fall off a cliff here. These same consensus scientists point to Crichton's twenty-page bibliography as being error-filled and distorted. A big part of our situation stems from oil spills, ones like your company foisted on the planet. You have made an oil slick out of the Gulf of Mexico. You even convinced President Obama to buy that technology would prevent any disaster in drilling. Wrong!

CM: Already the American people are waking up to the Obama baloney. He is a traitor to our American way of life. He wasn't even born in America.

PM: I can't believe you are aligning yourself with the Limbaughs and the Palins. You were a bright and shining young Democrat when we were in school. By the way, Hawaii, where Obama was born, is in America.

There you have a negative bonding pattern, a smoldering fire ignited by what? By vulnerability. Look on the surface, and you see no vulnerability. Both men zing each other, but profound vulnerability lurks beneath the surface in each man.

CM has worked hard to get to the top of his business. He has accrued wealth for a comfortable life style, and he is frankly frightened by the strange message he hears from his old friend. Just when he thought he had life knocked, his friend keeps telling him about a looming catastrophe.

PM has just returned from a seminar on the unfolding climate crisis. The presentations there terrified him. James Lovelock, the noted systems scientist, predicted the death of five billion people in the next thirty years. That's most likely an exaggeration growing out of Lovelock's disillusionment.[2] Still, PM can't imagine a scenario with even a million humans dying in a natural catastrophe. He really hasn't faced the profound terror he feels for himself and his grandchildren.

Neither of these men is fully aware of his vulnerability, so each attacks the other in a sarcastic, kidding way. Make no mistake: they are out for eventual blood.

> *"The release of atom power has changed everything except our way of thinking... the solution to this problem lies in the* **heart of mankind.** *(Author's emphasis) If only I had known, I should have become a watchmaker."*
>
> Albert Einstein

We will track this bonding pattern in the following chapters. The point at this moment is to notice the hidden vulnerability in both as the match lighting the fire. *Such ignition by vulnerability is almost always the case in conflict.*

Reduction of conflict (and war) lies in the direction of taking care of vulnerability in the heart of humans, beginning with ourselves.

17

Power Selves in the Council

Return to the discussion of the warrior selves in the council, or, as this chapter title describes, the power selves. Take a moment and scan your inner council. Who sits in prominent places? These power selves generally are the most obvious members of the inner council. They operate the inner auto by steering the interior council down life's road, and thus they are often called *the operating ego*.

As we evolve in childhood, this team of power selves develops to protect our vulnerability from the external environment. Their primary strategy lies in the use of control. They attempt to control the inner council and the outer environment all in the name of our personal safety and well-being.

This is the grand illusion in life: we imagine this operating ego of power selves as constituting *who we are*. We become so identified with this aspect of the inner council that we don't

> The non-dual (integral) mystic sees the operating ego (and the power selves) linked to the soul/essence. In this approach the ego is not the illusion per se. The soul is not the illusion. The illusion lies in thinking one or the other is the only reality. Authentic power lies in the integral path.

unfold into our deeper identity. We don't see the hidden potential of the soul/essence. Our true identity hides in the shadows of our council.

Who are these power sub-selves sitting inside us? The ones who speak the most frequently in our inner council are: the critic, the judge, the pusher, the perfectionist, the pleaser, the persecutor, the victim, the rescuer, the pleaser, the top dog, the under dog, and a whole host of others. A minor cast also bobs to the surface to make life interesting.

Why do the power selves think they are mainly who we are? These power selves developed, as was said earlier, with the aim of keeping the vulnerable selves safe. In most cases they forget (in a terrible forgetting) that their function is to protect our soft underbelly and *support the soul's journey*. Sadly, they often end up seeking control for control's sake, forgetful as they are. In this pattern they are spring-loaded for conflicts called negative bonding patterns, to which we now turn.

18

Negative Bonding Patterns Between Councils

Take the example of the negative bonding pattern between Mr. CM and Mr. PM. In the conversation presented, these men have little awareness of their vulnerability. They think the main point of their bonding is to see who wins the argument. The reward they seek is not nourishment or safety but the heroin-like high of being *right*.

CM's power selves bond with PM's vulnerable selves by hitting them with ridicule in comments about Al Gore. PM's power selves bond with CM's vulnerable selves by hitting them with comments about Limbaugh and Palin. *The bonding is in the hitting.* Unfortunately, this negative bonding is the typical male (and more recently, female) bonding seen in conversations like this one and eventually all the way to Congress. Congress has been in a massive negative bonding pattern for decades, and this partisan conflict may lay the groundwork for the extinction of the species.

Look at another classic negative bonding pattern seen in Greek narratives. Many of us, who cut our teeth on the classic saga of Socrates, saw him as the victim of the persecuting machine of the ignorant citizens of Athens.

Classics scholar, Jim Garrison, sees it in a more complex light. He addresses this question: Why, in a society enjoying more freedom and democracy than any the world had ever seen, would a seventy-year-old shaman/philosopher be put to death for what he was teaching?[1] Why, indeed!

Here is the context of the negative bonding pattern that resulted in Socrates' death. Socrates grew up during perhaps the first burst of democratic liberalism in the 200,000-year human story, as advocated by the statesman, Pericles. Pericles created the people's courts and used the public treasury to develop the arts. He instituted courts having 500 common people who sat on the court by means of drawing straws. They also drew straws to see who would be the judge. This arrangement evidently made Socrates very nervous. In a lawsuit you might draw someone who had no knowledge of the law as the judge in your case. In this Greek democracy your judge could be a farmer or a tanner of hides.

In such a situation Socrates must have felt very vulnerable, though he did not show it to the outside world in a direct way. He contemptuously criticized the right of every citizen to speak in the Athenian assembly. He expressed his unpopular views disdainfully and with an air of condescension. Laertius, a historian of the Third Century BCE, described the citizen response to Socrates thus, "...men set upon him with their fists or tore his hair out."[2] In general, people don't like it when you disrespect them and tell them they are incompetent buffoons.

In addition, two of Socrates' most famous students—Critias and Alcibiades—led Athens into war, corruption, and destruction. In this view of the Socratic story, the people of Athens naturally saw Socrates as a corrupting influence of their young people since two of their finest learned the Socratic Method. Application of that method led these former students to perdition, and, in turn, they ushered Athens to the brink of utter destruction.

The trial of Socrates was a massive negative bonding pattern that started out as an attempt to protect Athens from arrogant Socratic students who did not respect the common people. Many of Socrates' students evidently believed in ruling by central authority, not democracy. They didn't like the notion of checks and balances. When given power, they—at least in two prominent cases—abused it.

Like many negative bonding patterns, the fire of the countless inner councils of the Athenians raged in conflict until it resulted in the violence and ultimately death of Socrates. However, don't think Socrates was a victim or a martyr for the higher good. He, like most of us, promoted a massive negative bonding pattern through actions growing out of his unconscious or unaware state. We shall explore in a moment what his shadow might have been and why it resulted in his death.

In a startling demonstration of the human condition, Socrates brought about his own downfall through his—dare I say it? —ignorance of himself; namely, his refusal to own his vulnerability, and beyond even his vulnerability, his shadow.

As best I can tell from reading the mythic narratives, Socrates refused to look at himself, or at least his part in the bonding patterns he generated. He assumed he had the truth. His stated value was *truth pursued*, but his practice—in this crucial case—was *truth possessed*. At the end of the day, he knew the *truth*. The *he* I refer to here are the power selves in his inner council. In my reading of the accounts, he doesn't so much listen to the perspective of others as he provokes them toward a worldview he sees in advance. *Truth* here refers to Socrates' own agenda, or least the position of his power selves.

> **Truly, Socrates demonstrated his own mantra: the unexamined life is not worth living. Negative bonding patterns in their extreme result in violence and death, as exemplified with Socrates' choosing to drink the hemlock.**

Before I am assaulted by a host of Socratic scholars claiming I don't know what I am talking about, let me acknowledge the limitations of my telling of the story. I approach Socrates not as a psychological case study in historical time

> *"Aristophanes portrays Socrates as 'stalking the streets' and 'rolling his eyes' at remarks he found to be unintelligent."*
> Clouds, *A Play* 432 BCE

but rather as a myth probing the psycho/spiritual condition. We have little if any confirmation of the historicity of any of these accounts. I take the Socratic story as an archetypal telling of what I am calling negative bonding patterns between people's inner councils. I could easily follow the typical telling of the story and highlight Socrates' transcendent and aware-go moments, as do most professors of philosophy. Actually, I find my telling of the story as more interesting and, certainly, more human.

Now, we turn to see what fuels these intense conflicts, once they start.

19

Hidden Selves as Fuel in the Council

Go back to the fire in Chapter 16 for a moment. It is now burning, as is the fire of the negative bonding pattern. Remember, the tipi of juniper twigs, dry grass, and combustible mulch burn up very quickly. If the fire does not receive additional fuel, it will burn out without much harm. Any fire needs more substantial fuel in order to grow. So it is with negative bonding patterns between councils.

The shadow or hidden selves projected into the conversation provide the fuel. They are the new logs added to the fire. They are the hot wind blowing the fire out of control. The selves not fitting the values of our operating egos are disowned and hidden from our awareness. They are the ones most likely to get us into conflict with others. They are disowned or hidden from our awareness. Our operating egos

> Any judgment or criticism you have of another alerts you to the possibility of a negative bonding pattern. Why? These judgments are usually projections you don't like in yourself, so you thrust them onto other people in order not to have them in your council. *They taste bad; you spit them out. Then, you pretend the spit is not yours.*

don't like them because in the past they tended to get us into trouble in some way or at least that was our fear.

The bonfires of our conflicts require our shadows to continue.

Let's see how the fuel of hidden selves adds to the negative bonding pattern examples.

Mr. Corporate Man spends his life in the rough and tumble world of corporate work. He has pushed aside his sensitive selves that connect him to the environment. When he was a boy, he wandered through the woods and swam in a nearby river with PM. He loved Nature in its wildness. Slowly, in his adult life he disowned these Nature-based selves until they no longer had a place in his council. As he listened to PM, he felt these Nature-based selves creep back into his council. They were not welcome. If he accepted them, how could he continue in the work of the corporation? So, he spit them out.

He had selves sitting in his council who knew how his corporation would view such Nature-based selves. If these Wild Heart selves were accepted into the council, they might threaten his livelihood. So, his inner judge projected these environmental selves onto PM. Once out there, CM could make fun of them by pairing them with Al Gore. The more he made fun of PM, the less chance his own shadows had to speak in his inner council.

PM also has a shadow. When he hears CM speak of doubts about the data on the climate warming, he feels a rumbling in his own shadows about his own inner doubts. He gives lectures about climate warming. His operating ego mind is closed to new data that could have opposing information. He has written books on the subject. He thinks he is right.

What about his doubts? His questioning of the party line of environmentalists has no place in his inner council. To make certain his shadow doesn't sit down in his council, he spits his questioning of his own position out on CM, telling CM he is lost in denial about the climate crisis. "Only an idiot would deny climate warming." Like Socrates, he rolls his eyes at such stupidity.

In this state he is no longer a scientist but a scientific dogmatist. He has lost touch with the surprising, recuperative powers of

Nature to heal herself in spite of human bungling. Could Mother Earth have a strategy in mind to handle the current dire situation? Could she provide a small creature to eat our refuse?

In his dogmatic perspective PM might miss such a possibility. There is another shadow PM projects on CM: his own inner petro-chemical consumer. PM drives a car, flies all around the globe, doesn't change his life style all that much, and has a substantial carbon footprint. This consumer of petro-chemical products doesn't fit PM'S operating ego, so he projects that self onto CM. In this projecting, he doesn't have to deal with this shadow. He can feel the warmth of self-righteousness. In the scenario he builds in his own mind, Mr. CM is the bad guy destroying the planet while he, PM, is the good guy saving the human race.

> *"At the base of this ecosystem (volcanic vents in the deep canyons of the Caribbean) are chemical-eating bacteria that draw on the hydrogen sulfide and methane erupting from the vents to make food."*
>
> Jon Copley, Marine Biologist[1]

Each time these two friends feel the fire dying down in their negative bonding pattern, they project the above-mentioned shadows on each other. The fire then flares forth again. The shadows come from outside their awareness. As Jung commented, "The thing about the unconscious is it is unconscious."

Now, let's examine Socrates in his mythic negative bonding pattern. Keep in mind I am reading between the lines and treating Socratic stories as template myths. Among Socrates' accusers, one stands out, Anytus. In his relationship with Socrates, Anytus felt vulnerable for a number of reasons. First, he was a common man, a tanner of hides, and Socrates had little use for so-called common men, especially if they did not engage in his form of dialogue.

Next, Socrates' student, Plato's cousin Critias, became a political force in Athens, banished 5000 women from the city, and executed 1,500 of Athens's most prominent democrats. In his book, The *Trial of Socrates*, scholar I.F. Stone, points out that Socrates did nothing to stop the violence. Socrates was not bashful to speak out on a variety of subjects, but he was silent when it came to the violent misdeeds of his students. This chaos caused by Critias most assuredly affected Anytus' small business.[2]

But that wasn't the half of it. In the *Meno* Plato reports a relationship between Socrates and Anytus's beloved, young son. It may well have been sexual. Further, Socrates urged Anytus's son not to "continue in the servile occupation (of tanning hides) that his father provided for him."[3] What father likes for another man to guide his son away from the father's dreams? No wonder Anytus was ignited into the fire of conflict with this matrix of vulnerability.

Look at the Socratic side of the conflict. We can assume Socrates experienced considerable vulnerability about his trial and possible death. As far as I know, no reference is made to Socrates' inevitable vulnerability. Did his self-examination miss his vulnerability, a point I made earlier? What human does not feel vulnerable in the face of death? In projecting himself as the wisest man in Athens, does he overlook this very human fear? Certainly, Jesus found his own vulnerability in a similar situation at the last moment when he cried out with a sense of being forsaken.

These are a few of the vulnerabilities in both Socrates and Anytus, and now for the shadows fueling the negative bonding pattern.

What are the shadows Anytus projects onto Socrates? What did Anytus keep hidden from his own council's awareness? His courage to question, his confidence verging on arrogance, and his teaching abilities for his son come to mind. These are qualities Anytus and others hated in Socrates as indicated in the trial. On Socrates side, shadows that come to mind might be his feeling of compassion for the masses, his patience in tedious tasks like tanning hides, and his restraint and conscience in his sexuality with children. Knowing that Socrates lived in a culture whose values included sex with children does not diminish the darkness of this shadow.

Socrates negative bonding pattern with Anytus was just one of a network of bonding patterns he had with a variety of Athenians. These smaller bonfires conflagrated into a raging fire eventually consuming both Socrates and the 500 jurors, indeed all Athens. The result of this network of negative bonding patterns is, as they say, history. Well, not quite history since the facts elude us. Nevertheless, it is one of the compelling narratives in the entire human epic. I like this telling of the Socratic story because I so readily see myself mirrored.

Now, let's extend this model to include humans as they bond with larger Nature. Regarding the environmental crisis, we have a dominant culture in perpetual negative bonding with the Earth. We humans are quite vulnerable as a species. Have I emphasized this situation enough? Just listen to the negative bonding that appears when we talk about "getting hit hard" by a storm. As the climate heats up, we become more vulnerable about our very survival, and this vulnerability, disowned, ignites the fire of the negative bonding pattern. With the increasing intensity and wildness of the storms, we project our own wildness as a shadow on the weather.

In this vein hearken to just a handful of names we give to beautiful places in the wilds of North America: Hells Bay, Devil's Backbone, Devil's Punch Bowl, Devil's Playground, Devils Kitchen, Devil's Tower, Devil's Gorge, Hell Hole, Devils' Belt, Devil's Dripping Pan, Hell's Hollow Brook, Devil's Wharf, and Devil's Plunge. The primordial mind gave names of beauty to such places. In our dominant culture we often repress the experience of profound beauty and mystery, so we demonize the natural place with a negative name. It is our strange way of trying to control ourselves and the environment.

A common response of any ongoing negative bonding pattern sees a person tighten control over his situation as best he can. The knee-jerk behavior with melting glaciers, droughts, floods, monster storms, pollution, trash, and over-population is seen in this frenzy of control. Our dominant culture, seen at a distance, is a control freak.

A startling image of this control gone amuck is painted by John McPhee in his book, *The Control of Nature.*[4] He describes a situation in Iceland where the capital city, Reykjavik, has a wonderful deep water port. However, the humans there have a problem. Nearby volcanoes threaten to erupt, resulting in a worst case scenario of filling the deep water port with ash and magma. Naturally, the people and economy nudge into vulnerability. Their resulting strategy? They pump ice water out of the deep water port into the volcano in an attempt to keep the volcano from erupting.

What an image: a fire truck pumping cold water into a volcano. As I write, the volcano erupts and grounds air flight throughout Europe. Truth be told: we are helpless before even minor shifts in the Earth's crust.

Our puny and often misguided control efforts with the wildness of Nature points us in two other directions, to which we will now attend.

20

Enamored Councils:
Positive Bonding Patterns

A first cousin of a negative bonding pattern is a positive bonding pattern. Let's see what I mean.

Female meets male. Sparks fly. Chemistry happens. Whirlwind romance ignites. Birds and bees fly. Endless romantic comedies ensue. Such a process is Nature's way of getting relationships started. It's wonderful. It's exhilarating. It's sexy. It's fun. It's like being on an extended vacation. It's better than drugs.

A world-class artist sat in the car with me on his sixty-eighth birthday. His art was selling well. His health, good. He was attractive with gray, hair and beard, outlined against beautiful African American skin. He had a live-in partner of fifteen years and a relationship that, for all appearances, was positive and fulfilling. We were on our way to an outdoor experience to celebrate his special day.

"Edward," I asked him, "What would you like to do on the next leg of your journey?"

Wistfully, he answered, "I'd like to fall in love one more time before I die. I want to feel that high run through my body to my art." He longed for the *high* of intense, positive bonding.

In positive bonding patterns, a powerful attraction arises in one inner, sacred council to bond with another sacred council. The phrase—bonding pattern—refers to an energetic exchange between a person and the outside world taking the form of parent/child or power/vulnerability. The bonding repeats until it forms a grove or pattern etched in the personality so deep it defies change.

This positive bonding pattern can occur between the inner council of any person with another person's inner council. The pattern can happen in marriage, in friendship, with your house, your pet, your auto, your computer, your school, your nation, and with any aspect of the environment, including the wilderness.

Examples:

- A woman bonds positively between her inner child and a significant man (good father) to change the oil in her car.

- A man bonds positively between his inner child and a woman (good mother) to wash his clothes.

- Both bond positively with the garden at their new house.

While attractive, pleasant, pleasurable, and workable for some limited period of time, positive bonding patterns are often confused with intimacy. We shall look momentarily at the difference between the two and the deeper meaning of intimacy. Meanwhile, consider the following points.

> **ALERT! Positive bonding patterns (+bp) switches easily to negatives (−bp.) WHY? +bp covers up issues that then erupt in the switch to −bp.**

The **SWITCH** happens quickly.

Consider the romantic +bp where the play-by-the rules woman is attracted to and bonded with the freedom loving, bad boy with a motorcycle. He is exciting, unpredictable, and sexy. His wild child challenges her usual, staid parental stance in a wild ride that lasts for months. Then, comes the switch from +bp to −bp. Hal and Sidra Stone call this moment a **SLAP**, because the switch slaps both inner councils in the face.[1] Suddenly, to the woman, the wild, bad boy is the irresponsible man. She can't stand him. The delightful challenge of thrilling the prim and proper woman becomes a shock to the man who now sees her as a critical *bitch*. He can't stand her. *The very bond that attracted them becomes the dynamic slapping them in the face.*

Such a similar switch often happens with the environment. A person lies in the warm sun on a mountainside looking forward to a weekend of relaxing camping. The positive bonding is exquisite. Then comes the summer thunderstorm, and the inner council of the person curses the ecological council—or weather system—making what was pleasurable into conflict and pain. We bond positively with the soft breezes of New Orleans, until we realize a Katrina lurks in the Gulf.

Then, comes the **slap**. What we loved, we now grumble about, even hate. These moments grab us and shake our romantic notions about the Nature-based selves with a passion. On the other hand: Is it not true we remember the challenging moments in Nature while camped out, even more than we remember pleasurable ones?

Such a **switch** is currently happening with our dominant American culture and the environment in general. For example, we have lived for a century in a +bp between humans, autos, and open roads across America, the beautiful. *Oh, for the lure of the open road.* It seemed like an always available pattern made in heaven. In fact, one version of Heaven in the Bible encour-

> The scripture of the Bible and the Scripture of Nature seemed to be bonded positively through the first two centuries of American history, but now the two scriptures are in conflict. (-bp) We are in the midst of a rude awakening. Nature's new scripture is currently being written. It transcends the earlier plea for human dominion. The Scripture of Nature is inspired by the Holy Spirit. Let those who have ears to hear and eyes to see pay close attention. Look at chapter and verse in the melting glaciers, clogged cities, and plastic laden oceans. Memorize the oil slick in the Gulf.

ages us to "…let them (humans) have dominion over the fish of the sea, and over the fowl of the air, and over the cattle, and over all the earth." (Genesis 1:26)

The **switch** smacks us in the face. In recent times we filled the air with carbon dioxide (CO_2). Why would we engage in such outrageous practices? Is it the result of the Biblical command? We bonded with the Earth as controlling masters just as scripture instructs. Currently, the human role of dominion, **switches** to reveal our possible destruction as victims. Nature slaps us in the face to reveal the error of our ways. All the signs alert the human species, "You must change or die."

Beyond negative and positive bonding patterns emerges the possibility of intimacy.

21

The Intimate Council

In a recent lecture Brian Swimme, mathematical cosmologist, pondered the scientific discovery of the expanding Universe. Many questions arise with this discovery. If the Universe is expanding, into what domain is it expanding?[1] The word, *Universe*, implies everything exists within it, yet there must be something else because said Universe is expanding into something.

That mind twister prepares us for a second and more important question. Accept as a given, the *Universe is expanding*. Einstein proposed this paradigm-shattering truth, and the Hubble telescope eventually supported the notion.[2] This simple statement has become the basis of modern astronomy and, indeed, space travel itself.

If the Universe is expanding or moving toward some point, *what is the point*? Expanding implies *toward* or *direction*. The point of the expansion leads to what paleontologist, Teilhard de Chardin, describes as *the Omega Point*.[3] Bravely, Swimme offers a clear and concise description of what he proposes the point to be. His hypothesis arises after decades of astronomical observation.

"The Universe is moving in the direction of reaching a point where every aspect of the Universe knows every other aspect in its depth."[4]

This observation, based on decades of Swimme's research, startles on many levels, not the least of which is its implication. ***Such a statement implies the point of life: intimacy.***

If so, what is this illusive experience called intimacy?

> After the 8.8 magnitude earthquake in Chile on February 27, 2010, scientists tell us the quake shifted the axis of the Earth. The shift shortens each day on Earth by 1.28 microseconds. Whatever happens anywhere touches us all, *intimately.*

To address this question of intimacy, return for a moment to Chapter 12, *The Amazing Aware-Go*, so we can unpack the question of intimacy.

First, intimacy requires that we acknowledge our many selves. Pressure and stress in our life conditions commands us to be able to pull off whatever sub-self is stuck to the Velcro of our chests. These sub-selves try to relieve the pressure of daily life but often end up adding to the problem.

How does dislodging them help? The aim is to view any sub-self with neutrality. Intimacy in its initial stages requires an upset of our usual stasis. Breaking out of our habits is a necessary prelude to intimacy. For instance, picture your inner critic stuck to your chest with Velcro. No matter what happens in a given situation, you feel the sometimes debilitating density of your critic on your breast. The weight of your inner critic is so close to you that you can't look at it. The criticism seeps in through your skin and surrounds your heart. A dislodging action is required in order to hold it in your hands at arm's length so you can look at it.

Second, we need to be able to move into that sub-self without getting lost in it. The task: be aware in the drama of the sub-self but not of it. Look at it compassionately but refuse its domination.

Third, we will need to discover the sub-self opposite of that sub-self and then hold the opposing forces in tension for the moment. Intimacy requires sitting quietly with the tension without panicking.

Fourth, we will need to ascend the mountain (or ladder) to the high place of the Witnessing Presence to view with neutrality the sub-selves in tension. This meditative state becomes of utmost importance because it is the gateway to the Witnessing Presence. A path to this state of consciousness is described in Chapter 10.

Fifth, we take this hard-earned awareness back into the space of the ego to form the aware-go. With regard to the *critical sub-self* the aware-go then has many choices that arise as a result of the hard-earned neutrality.

At this point, the stage for intimacy has been set. We are prepared to channel to the outside world what we have discovered in our inner council work.

Assume for a moment that another person engages in a similar exercise of examining his or her inner council in the way I just mentioned. You both want to talk to each other; you have the deeply felt urge to connect. The interfacing of these two aware-go councils constitutes what I call *intimacy. Intimacy at the higher levels of the human experiment is a profound merging of the aware-go's and their council.*

Such a process may sound impossibly complex. How could anyone ever achieve such an experience? Let's look at intimacy in action.

In 1969, I attended a workshop with the much respected psychologist Rollo May. Dr. May was reserved and dignified, as were most of the group of psychotherapists in the seminar. Halfway through May's formal presentation, a wild-looking man dressed in a dashiki stalked

> **When these interchanging moments occur, the Council bursts forth in all its glory as Sacred. The Council of selves is implicitly Sacred, but acts of intimacy make the Sacred explicit. In intimacy we are the Intimate Word of Life becoming flesh. We are the implicate Sacred becoming the explicate Sacred.**

into the room with his gray beard flapping against his chest. He didn't sit in a chair. He walked up to where the refined May was speaking and sat down in front of him on the floor cross-legged and defiant.

A buzz moved through the room, punctuated with gasps. Who was this wild man? Soon, he stood up, stretched, and said to May, "What you are saying is worse than bull shit. It is elephant shit."

The wild man, I later learned, was Fritz Perls, father of Gestalt Therapy. His wildness attracted me. Later, in further training experiences, I heard him offer his famous Gestalt prayer:

> *I do my thing,*
> *And you do your thing.*
> *I am not in this world to live up to your expectations.*
> *And you are not in this world to live up to mine.*
>
> *You are you,*
> *And I am I,*
> *And if by chance*
> *We find Each other,*
> *It is beautiful.*
>
> *If not, it can't be helped.*
>
> —Fritz Perls

Such a prayer is suggestive, if not sufficient, regarding intimacy. Fritz Perls was rude and wild. Rollo May was civil and reserved. They each did their thing. Fritz was a rule-breaker. Rollo, a rule keeper. Different, yet each had done his work in exploring the inner council. They clashed that day. They began in a negative bonding pattern. Like the rest of the Universe, they were, in that moment, messy. The situation was chaotic. They reeked of each other's shadows. They teetered on an explosion, provoked by both Perls' rule breaker and May's rule keeper.

Yet, to me, the situation was ripe with beauty. I sensed the

> *"Communication leads to community, that is, to understanding, intimacy, and mutual valuing.*
>
> *Hate is not the opposite of love; apathy is."*
>
> Rollo May,
> Personal Notes, 1969

potential of intimacy. Because each had heeded the sound of the conch of evolution and done their basic exploration of themselves, a kind of intimacy emerged out of the disorder of their conflict and crisis. The dance of their two councils

> *"My friends say I have a problem with intimacy. They don't know me that well."*
>
> Line from Saturday Night Live

was authentic. Their dialogue was transparent. May's face showed his vulnerability. Perls eventually moved away from his drama to reciprocity. Perls slapped May on the back and laughed loudly. May grinned. Perls yelled. May wrinkled his brow in contemplation. Perls shouted one-liners and poetry. May offered complexity in modulated tones. Time stood still.

Sometimes, their fighting was the drama of unaware sub-selves striking out at the other. At other moments their fighting was aware and honest disagreement. In some ways they met. In others they didn't. When they didn't, they both seemed content.

"And if we find each other, it is beautiful. If not, it can't be helped."

I came away from that day knocked off balance and, paradoxically, exhilarated. I saw that intimacy doesn't always mean being friendly, close, and warm. Sometimes, it means clashing. I hadn't thought of intimacy in that way.

Being intimate can mean closeness or distance.
It can mean loud or soft.
It can mean yelling or whispering.
It can mean intense feeling or quiet reflection.
It can mean tender sex or the ending of a relationship.
It can mean letting your boundaries go.
It can mean establishing clear boundaries.

The notion we are all intimately related emerges in consciousness very early in the human story. In fact, most of the indigenous

> Intimacy means channeling to the outside world what I think or feel through the aware-go. I trust you to do the same. If we meet, it is beautiful. We forge a different kind of connection by knowing each other more deeply. We become the Universe fulfilling its destiny of intimacy.

cultures start with that premise. Key words arise in early human language whose very sound carry the tones of intimacy.

In my formative years I learned about the Lakota expression—*mitakuye oyasin*. Literally, it means "all my relations." It is a prayer for oneness and harmony with all forms of life. When I hear that phrase from one of my fellows in the Earthtribe, an immediate intimacy occurs. This form of intimacy is native to all life; E.O. Wilson, the biologist, again assists us with his phrase—*biophilia*, or the love of life itself.[5]

To continue this exploration, take the Comanche word *puha*. I was taught early on that the word means, *The Sacred breathes through us a mighty power*. Or, *the Sacred Wind blows through all*. What a picture of intimacy: a Sacred Wind blowing through us all.

Pneuma is the ancient Greek word for *breath* or *wind*. Pre-Socratic shamans used the word to describe the animating, warm breath in both the cosmos and the body. This Greek word suggests the importance of our bodies in intimacy. Opening the body to allow Vital Life to flow through is the essence of physical intimacy. Such a practice is the soul of the truly erotic experience.

Apu is the Quechua (Inca) word for Life (Spirit) flowing from the mountains. In the Quechua language, still the native and first language of the Andes, there is no verb for *to have* or *to possess*. You don't have a horse; you are *with* or *related* to the horse. You don't own a computer; you are with a computer. You don't have a Spirit; you are related to Spirit. You don't have a dog or cat as a pet; you are companions, related. Apu passes between you. The Apu or mountain spirit is both with you and passes through you. *Quechua intimacy shouts the importance of reciprocity.*

Ruah is the Hebrew world for Vital Breath, wind, and air. It often denotes a puff of wind, and, not only wind in general, but a particular wind. Ancient Hebrew shamans were so intimate with the wind they could detect the differences of the energy in the types of wind. The King James Version of the Bible translates *Ruah* in this way: "And the Spirit of God (Ruah) moved upon the face of the waters." (Gen. 1:2,KJV) I prefer the shamanic and more ancient understanding of *Ruah*: "And the East Wind Spirit (Ruah) moved upon the face of the waters." The energetically sensitive Hebrew shaman knew intimately which wind did what.

The ancient shaman exhibited an intimacy with the ecology we have lost, as indicated by these words from the roots of the human story. If we are to survive and thrive as humans on planet Earth, we will need to dive deeply into the roots of the shamanic era and retrieve our soul connections, our intimacy with all forms of the Universe.

In the intimacy of this deep dive into the Mystery of the Wild lies our hope.

> *The most beautiful thing we can experience is the mysterious.*
>
> *It is the source of all true art and science.*
>
> Albert Einstein,
> *What I Believe*

After I had finished my doctoral studies and established a practice of psychotherapy, I noticed my clients were raising questions not within the purview of my training, a point I began with in the prologue of this book. After my clients moved through depression, or anxiety, or marital trouble, or an addiction, they would ask me, "What now?" I didn't have a clue. I had lost touch with my deepest essence as a person embedded in Nature. My twelve years of college and graduate study had somehow covered over and suffocated my soul rather than liberating my spiritual DNA.

> *"Ever more people today have the means to live, but no meaning to live for."*
>
> Viktor Frankl

I returned to tribal elders for what would become eight years of shamanic training, or what one of my teachers, Bear Heart, called "medicine man, traditionally trained." On one of our first training expeditions, he took me to a windy mesa in New Mexico. We sat for a long while, and then he spoke:

When I was three days old, my mother took me to a hilltop near our home and introduced me to the elements. First she introduced me to the Four Directions—East, South, West, and North.

Then, she prayed in a very intimate way,"I'm asking special blessings for this child. You surround our lives and keep us going. Please protect him and bring balance into his life."

Next, she touched my tiny feet to this Mother Earth.

"Dear Mother and Grandmother Earth, one day this child will walk, play, and run on you. I will try to teach him to have respect for you as he grows up. Wherever he may go, please be there supporting and taking care of him."

She lifted me up to be embraced by the breeze as she spoke. This place was in Oklahoma, so there was always a breeze.

"Please recognize this child. Sometimes you will blow strong, sometimes you'll be very gentle, but let him grow up knowing the value of your presence at all times as he lives on this planet."

What a beautiful moment for a baby to feel at three days old. I could see the intimacy in Bear Heart's eyes as he spoke. I was still in my young man years, and I yearned for the kind of intimacy he had with the wind and all elements of the environment. About twenty years later Molly Larkin would write his biography with the subtitle: *The Life and Teachings of a Native American Shaman.* Those words didn't quite suit Bear Heart. So, he suggested the title: *The Wind Is My Mother.*[6]

Thinking about what he said, I asked him, "If the wind is your mother, who is your father?"

"The Bear is my father, and one day I will tell you more about that."

And so, I began a forty-year journey to reclaim my indigenous self within the Primordial Mind, my heritage as a human, so absolutely necessary for my intimacy with the Universe. I began the soul/retrieval voyage to connect with that aspect in my inner council referred to by Bear Heart's biological mother and by the whisper of his ecological Mother, the Wind.

We all have an indigenous mind. If you follow your roots far enough back, you will find the indigenous self: perhaps, in Native America, or Europe, or the Middle East, or Africa. No inner council in this crucial time can be fully sacred without that indigenous self, child of the Primoridal Mind. Don't leave home without it.

When it came time to *baptize* my grandchildren, I remembered Bear Heart's Mother, both his biological mother and his Mother, the Wind. With the enthusiastic participation of our daughters and their husbands, Judith and I took our grandchildren out on the limestone hill where we live.

We laid down a buffalo robe and lifted the conch shell given to our family by my great grandmother. Through the shell we blew *puha, apu, pneuma, ruah,* the *Breath of Life.* I uttered words similar to Bear Heart's mother. I wanted our grandchildren to have in the cells of their bodies the sound of the wind and the magic of the conch shell. I wanted them to carry in their cells the sound of the conch and to feel its magical vibrations in their hearts—an intimacy with Nature. In short, I aspired for them to enter into *mitakuye oyasin,* or to know all in the Universe as their relatives.

If we recover this intimacy, then we will be saved as a species. If not, we will fade and go the way of the Neanderthals.

> "*If you bring forth what is inside you, what you bring forth will save you.*
>
> *If you don't bring forth what is inside you, what you don't bring forth will destroy you.*"
>
> Jesus, The Gospel of Thomas

Return to the fire on the cold morning mentioned earlier, the one where students from Wisdom University and the Earthtribe gathered. It was cold and rainy, not the kind of day for a picnic. Nevertheless, the participants gathered for soul/retrieval. They wanted to bring into their inner council an intimacy with the Environment they—like most of us—had lost through the dominance of our culture. They wanted—if even for a moment—to recover their connection with the Wild Heart.

I recalled Bear Heart's teaching. I told them we were only a breath away from our ancient, wilder selves. I told them the wind was always wild and could never be controlled by humans, no matter how hard we try. I told them we could bring these lost selves into our councils simply by coming out on a cold morning, standing around a fire, and feeling the wind on our faces.

In a Sacred Circle we joined our Sacred Inner Councils.

We chanted *Puha*, using the Comanche word. We inhaled as we touched the Earth and exhaled as we touched the sky.

We chanted *Apu*, using the Quechua word. We inhaled as we touched the Earth and exhaled as we touched the sky.

We chanted *Pneuma*, using the Greek word, also used in the New Testament. We inhaled as we touched the Earth and exhaled as we touched the sky.

We chanted *Ruah*, using the Hebrew word. We inhaled as we touched the Earth and exhaled as we touched the sky.

We chanted *Puha, Apu, Pneuma, Ruah*. We felt the connection of all these traditions as we inhaled and exhaled. They all had a similar sound.

In doing so, we vowed to make our Councils Sacred. We became Sacred by being intimate with all aspects of the Universe. We allowed this intimate connection to flow through us—around the circle and through our hearts—out to informal circles emerging throughout the planet.

Somewhere inside we knew we were discovering our true identities as relatives with all. We were taking a small step in the direction of Brian Swimme's vision of every aspect knowing every other aspect in its fullest.

This tender intimacy, this rambunctious wind, this gentle breathing all drew us into a powerful touching of our Wild Hearts—the crux of the Sacred Council.

PART IV

Wild Heart Stories
The Sacred Council Listens to Its Wild Side

*"What lies beyond us and what lies before us are
small matters compared to what lies within us."*
— Ralph Waldo Emerson

*"If you don't know the trees, you may be lost in the
forest, but if you don't know the stories, you may
be lost in life."*
— Siberian Elder

*"Sometimes a person needs a story more than food
to stay alive."*
— Barry Lopez

"If you keep telling the same, sad, small story, you will keep living the same, sad, small life."
— Jean Houston, Wisdom University

"To be a person is to have a story to tell."
— Isak Dinesen

22

The Power of Story

An osprey nest appears out of nowhere on the side of the road. It sits on the top of a telephone pole adjacent to the Umpqua River in Oregon. Locals tell me this fecund river provides the premier salmon run in the Northwest. The ospreys agree. Working on the platform is a handsome pair tending to their nest. Their energy reaches out to me. Stopping the car, I crane my neck and utter under my breath, "Are you Greek muses? Polyhymnia? Or Clio? Or maybe Erato? Or muses as yet unknown?" My utterance grows from a deep inspiration welling up out of mysterious depths.

This handsome pair of birds does not look anything like the usual rendition of Greek muses. Still the urge to tell a story concerning the hidden mystery of the power of love between humans and non-human creatures arises in me. A variety of inner selves rustle inside as the cries of the osprey call them forth. A sense of the glorious web existing between my inner council and the larger council of human and non-human beings beckons me, calling forth stories.

It is time to settle by a fire like the one mentioned earlier in this book. Join me, reader.

> "It takes a thousand voices to tell a single story."
>
> Bear Heart, Indigenous Shaman, Creek Tribe

It is a chilly night, and the warmth of the fire feels good as it searches out cold places in our hearts. With our bellies full of vegetarian chili and a blanket thrown over our shoulders, we can settle back to stories of the Sacred Web in search of hope and possibility.

23

A Story of Survival

This story occurs in a hotel in Oakland, California, The Washington Inn. I sit at the window early in the morning on a Friday of a seminar at Wisdom University, engaging in my morning meditation. As such, I have little connection in this urban setting with the wilder side of early humans as they evolved in Africa or with their daily challenges. For the moment I have lost a keen rapport with non-human creatures such as the osprey.

Air conditioning separates me from the surprises of Nature. Only a pigeon or two fly by distracting me from the noise of the trash collection trucks and the steady background hum of traffic. I am a fully modern human, quite distanced from our untamed forbearers. My big survival challenge of the day? A trip to Starbucks.

I notice a long line of people on the street below my window, each with a paper sack in his hands. I follow the line with my eye, and it leads to the back of a red and white, F-150 Ford pickup truck.

"What are these people doing in line so early in the morning?" I mumbled under my breath loud enough for Judith, my spouse, to answer me.

"I don't know," she says, distracted from dressing herself for the day by my mumbling.

As my eyes focus on the scene, I see a series of cages in the back of the rusting bed of the truck. A lone man reaches into the cages and extracts a living creature flopping around in his hands. From my second story room, I try to build a larger picture for what is increasingly an ominous circumstance. I gain momentary relief from anxious anticipation when I realize the truck is part of the Friday Farmer's Market. The people standing in line are mainly of Asian descent, and they are intent on buying whatever the man holds securely in his hands.

As my eyes hone in on the man, I can see something squirming, maybe a pigeon. The man twists and deftly breaks the neck of the bird, and places the limp body in his customer's paper sack.

As I look on, horrified at the raw loss of life, another bird escapes when the tall, gaunt man opens the next cage. The bird's topknot identifies the escapee as a quail. An overwhelming urge arises for me to rescue the bird, but it is too late. Before I can move to leave my room, passers-by capture the cute, little quail and take it back to its destiny with the executioner. He breaks the quail's neck and places it in a brown sack for a happy customer.

I pause here to remind myself, and you, kind reader, of my intention to tell a love story between human and non-human creatures with the aspiration that we humans can rekindle the flame in our hearts for the larger environment. How can this killing of bird after bird point to a love story?

With that question taunting me, I hear my childhood mother's voice instructing me in how to wring a chicken's neck, and then chop off the head. She showed me how to pick the feathers, and, later in the day, we ate the chicken.

My story seems stranger and stranger with the contrast of killing and pleasant memories. A warmth wells up in my heart at the memory of my mother's voice, even as she teaches me to kill a helpless creature. I could tell by a slight tremor in her hand that she was squeamish.

Then, I recall another facet of the story. As a boy I had a teacher who taught me how to ask permission of the bird when I killed it to eat. I learned the very act of killing could be a gesture of respect. I was taught to consult the Master of Animals in the Sacred Council of Beings if I wished to kill and then have food to eat. I learned that the non-human creature lives on through me and that one day my body would return to the Earth to feed it with my remains. The Indigenous Elder called this process the spiral of life.

My childhood, as I indicated earlier, came at the end of The Great Depression. The survival energy of early humans took hold powerfully as it does in any time when human survival is threatened. Such a time is upon us now in spades, and, perhaps, that is the reason the following part of the story comes to me.

My father and I hunted and shot the very bobwhite quail I wanted to save from having its neck broken in the Oakland market. We needed the meat for our survival in economically stressed times, though being an elementary age boy, I didn't understand such matters. My seeing the pigeons and the quail being killed on that Friday morning rubber banded me back into the primal wisdom of early humans and their relatives, the creatures they hunted. Deep in my heart I felt the profound tie between hunter and hunted. As human beings we have the capacity to kill and to eat with love and respect for the bounty of the Earth. We are of the Earth, not over the Earth.

Eat with love and respect.

Eat with love and respect.

Eat with love and respect.

The gift of the first stage of human evolution is the very deep connection between predator and prey. This vital connection merits the word love. A blessed tie binds our Wild Hearts with ordinary life in this primordial act in life's cycle.

24

A Story of Allies in the Council

Lisa works as an assistant police chief in San Marcos, Texas. She commands eighty police persons and is in charge of an award winning approach to trauma in this city, home to Texas State University, a fast

> *"Life will go on as long as there is someone to tell stories and to listen."*
>
> Oren Lyons, Iroquois Elder, Onondaga Reservation

growing institution of some 30,000 students. Stress abounds in her job.

This particular story began with her decision to go on a vision quest in the New Mexico mountains with Judith and me. I use the term vision quest here to describe an experience of meditating in the wilderness over a period of days.

The first challenge in the retreat was a considerable climb up a mountain, past a beautiful, coldwater spring, to a high meadow. Typical of her life style, Lisa pushed even farther up the mountain to pitch her tent and begin her meditation quest, one where she fasted and slept on the ground seeking an "enlargement of her soul," as Plato put it.[1]

Even though the days were warm with July sun, the nights saw the temperature plunge to near freezing, cold enough to get your attention in summer sleeping gear. Understandably, the stress of the mountain coupled with the accumulated stress of 24-7 crime stopping in a suburban city combined to drive Lisa to distraction. *Distraction* describes her life and the rest of us as well.

Her busy mind flitted back and forth between the responsibilities of her job and the rock under her back as she tried to sleep. She obsessed with the thought of moving her tent to a better place. Nothing was happening, and she felt a rising frustration with the situation. Perhaps, the Master of the Council of Animals slept and had forgotten her. Or maybe the Master whispered in her ear, "Not to worry. Not to worry. Magic is just around the corner."

The next morning the sun flowed into her tent warming her chilled and throbbing feet. Lisa unzipped the flap, meditated, and prayed as best she could. Her prayer aimed at opening herself to the beautiful wilds all around. Some small awakenings started to happen, but not in her conscious mind. Nature worked with her through her limbic system as it tuned into the Primordial Wisdom latent in the mountain meadow.

She felt warm rays. She breathed fresh, mountain air. She relaxed. Time passed. Still *nothing* happened, at least according to her usual operating ego. She peered through the flap of her tent, thinking of taking the short trip out of the civilization of the tent to the wilds beckoning to her. She closed her eyes to get a few moments of sleep in the warmth of the day.

Then, she heard a sound—a low, growling, a whirling, a presence. Her eyes opened. There in the tent with her buzzed a ruby throated hummingbird.

Time stopped.

Another form of time, eternal in quality, descended on the tent as if to say, "If you won't come to me, I will come to you."

The hummingbird came closer, then even closer. Lisa barely breathed. The bird flitted to her face as if looking her in the eye. Then, with a gesture impossible to miss even by the most skeptical, the creature moved in and inserted its bill into a nostril. After a moment, it withdrew only to touch her tanned cheek as if in a kiss.

The stress of myriad unsolved crimes drained away. The pains of her body faded. The thoughts of her rental property receded. Nothing in the Universe existed except her and the gentle touch of the bird, a mysterious touch of the hand of the Sacred Mystery.

In that moment she joined hands with the spiritual impulse of 200,000 years of the human epic. The bill of the tiny bird linked her inner council with the larger Council of All Beings, the Wild Heart of The Primordial. The magic of the mountain ecology invaded her as if to say, "Our job is to assist you in being awake, aware, and alive. The Earth has a vested interest in your awakening. You are needed in this time of crisis. Your particular form of awareness, choices, and practices will see humans through the darkness of this moment in our beautiful blue Earth Being."

The ally touches to awaken.

The ally touches to awaken.

The ally touches to awaken.

> This stage is the second phase of the evolutionary story of humans. The gift of this shamanic era is the loving awakening touch of non-human creatures who seek to elicit an evolving love story between all elements of the the Earth with humans. Indigenous people call these helpers—*allies*. Greeks call them muses. Christians call them angels. Scientists call them *fractals* from the morphogenic field.

25

A Story of Wild Heart Community

A truck fitted for large animals rolled into the ceremonial meadow of Deer Dancer Ranch just outside Columbus, Texas. Elders in the spiritual community, the Earthtribe, blindfolded Judith and me and asked us to sit quietly, explaining they had a surprise for us. I heard a banging on the sideboards coming from the truck, along with raucous sounds I couldn't quite name.

Once the truck driver turned off the engine, the elder took the blindfolds off, and we beheld a tumultuous scene. Some wild creature bounced back and forth in the closed bed of the truck, tipping it first in one direction and then another. The truck driver set up a plank leading from the bed of the truck to the ground and threw open the doors. Out shot a shaggy creature, frothing at the mouth.

It was a young buffalo, colloquial for the American bison. Just that morning she was weaned from her mother, and she was not a happy camper. The elders explained with joy they were giving this young buffalo to Judith and me as a gift in appreciation for our years of service and leadership.

What a beautiful gesture it was!

However, the young buffalo was not having any part of it. Throwing her head first one way and then another, slobber flung in every direction. Her wild eyes searched for her lost mother.

"Who were these strange beings in a circle around the truck?" She might ask.

I didn't know what to do. Then, I recalled a vision song given to our tribe to be sung to the buffalo council out of respect for all they have done for humans in North America:

> Yaka Bah, Yaka Bah,
> Yenasaw ain Yaka Bah,
> Yenasaw ain Yaka Bah,
> Yaka Bah, Yaka Bah

Roughly translated:

> Buffalo, Buffalo,
> I walk with you,
> Hand on your hump,
> Buffalo, Buffalo

The meaning of the words took a backseat to the resonant energy spiraling through our bodies. Deep from within we sent sound waves to the frothing buffalo, straight to the limbic system of her mammalian brain. Her eyes relaxed. She reached a still point. Soon, she settled down and walked slowly toward the circle and our smiling faces. Her massive chest held a good heart radiating friendly energy toward us. In that moment she bonded with us as her herd, her community, and we, with her.

For the next year she listened for us when we arrived each month for the tribal gathering. Soon, she made her way to stand near our circle when we would council. Sometimes, we could hear her breathing outside the sweat lodge. Buffalo have double lungs developed evolutionarily to enable them to run long distances across the prairie, so she breathed in a distinct manner, rumbling her energy through our community.

With 500 acres of free range on the ranch for roaming, she happily wandered to her Wild Heart's content. However, the remuda of horses didn't really accept her, nor the heard of red deer, nor any of the other creature families. Although she loved being with her human family, her downcast energy told us she needed something more. Being part of our human tribe wasn't enough. We were companions but not her herd. To discover her natural and true identity and radiate her natural wisdom she needed a herd.

Responding to her need, we purchased her a male companion, and her energy immediately changed. They entered a positive bonding pattern, and, I hazard to guess, a form of intimacy unique to their species. Time passed. She and her mate birthed a fine calf. Our beloved friend drifted away from our human tribe because she was finding her true nature within her own kind.

Soon her herd found their way into our Sacred Council gatherings through our various ceremonies. The human council and the buffalo council lived collaboratively for years until she died giving birth.

Because of her influence, our Earthtribe experimented with retrieving the soul expanding practice of our indigenous ancestors of eating buffalo meat, especially during high ceremonies. Even some of our vegetarians found this practice to expand consciousness as we ingested the power and wisdom of these ancient ones. After eating this very healthy and lean meat, we seemed to be able to look through the complex issues of our personal and global crises.

The meat gave us the Third Eye of the Wild Heart.

Not long ago I took my grandson, Will, to see the original buffalo's grandson on the ranch. Will and I sat on our haunches and sang the same song we had sung to our buffalo friend on the morning of her arrival. A profound sense of companionship settled over us. We were one with her, her grandson, and all humans who had been nourished by the gifts of the buffalo to our lives through the ages. Intimacy between grandfather, grandson, and all living creatures moved through us as we experienced buffalo's wildly beating heart. For one grand moment our domesticity was balanced by the wild. We had an urge to touch the magnificent being, but we knew he remained untamed.

We spoke of how the buffalo symbolizes the vast resources of the Earth, its ability to Self-organize, its current vulnerability, and our responsibility to do our part. We spoke of how these wonderful creatures on the ranch live on the boundary between the wild and the domestic. We spoke of how they can guide us to live our own lives on this perilous boundary. We spoke of how these glorious creatures had reached the edge of extinction and therfore possess wisdom for us in the current state of our species. We spoke this phrase:

> We can be both wild and tame.
> We can be both wild and tame.
> We can be both wild and tame.

This story encompasses at least two orbits of the spiral of evolution: the magic and the mythic structures of consciousness. As evolution unfolded, both humans and other non-human creatures found a way to be companions. We cannot survive during this planetary crisis without such co-operative companionship. We must return to these indigenous practices, for in them rests the key to the larger human story.

26

A Story of the Council of Fire and Water

A dreamy young man sought a path through the chaos of his father's business failure and the tension between his parents, thoroughly modern people with marital and financial stress. The business failure forced a move to a foreign country to make ends meet. The year was 1895.

> *"Our species thinks in metaphors and learns through stories."*
>
> Mary Catherine Bateson, physician, quoting her father, Gregory Bateson, anthropologist

The young man's dream was to attend a school for electrical engineers, a career emulating his father. However, he failed the entrance exam. No one was particularly surprised at his failure because he learned to talk later than most and didn't excel in school when he did learn to talk.

Upon being rejected by the school of his dreams, he found a very ordinary university where he explored a problem niggling the edges of his mind. As a youngster he recalled sitting on a hill and watching a train approaching, from left to right. The train blew its whistle as it approached. The sound was faint. As the train came closer, the sound grew louder. As the train passed and disappeared into the distance, the sound grew fainter.

He examined his experience of the train. The sound waves were not constant. They were relative to the position of the train as related to his position on the hillside. The paradigm of physics in the late 1800's offered some help, but could not explain fully the relativity of his experience.

Once out of graduate school, he moved to Switzerland and applied for a teaching position at Zurich University. Again, he failed to get the position of his blissful dreams and took a lesser job as a clerk at a patent office. By now, you may have guessed this young man was Albert Einstein. You probably also know he continued to puzzle over the issue of relativity.

What you may not know is the source of his inspiration, or how the ally, or muse, or angel, or fractal appeared to him. What means would this organism called Earth, use to enter Albert's consciousness on behalf of the larger story?

Albert made close friends in Zurich. He drew them into a discussion concerning the niggling problem of the relativity of time and space as exemplified in his childhood experience of the sound of the train. Often, he and his friends hiked into the Swiss Alps with this topic on their minds. Sometimes, they hiked as far as eighteen miles until they came to a crystal clear lake. There, they pitched their tents and built a fire.

Time and again, they repeated this hike. They sometimes swam in the icy water, and dried off next to a roaring fire. As they sat warming their hands by the fire, their dialogue expanded into areas previously unexplored by any humans at any time. They stared into a fire within the fire, "the fire that takes no wood, a fire that burns in the Mystery."[1] They didn't build this inner fire; it built them. On these hikes the fire gave them a flame of the mind that could not be extinguished.

Their inner councils mingled with a chain of human councils through the millennia, all inspired by fire and water. Albert looked deeply into the fire. He slept on the ground. He bathed in the water. He sailed across the face of the lake. He took notes on the visions unfolding through the Sacred Council of Beings into areas forbidden by the scientific models of his day.

He distilled his findings into four short papers, aided by the mathematics of his fellow council members. In 1905, he presented his papers. The world was largely silent; few understood. The first paper explored the nature of light and how it flows in discrete packets called quanta. Was this paper the fire itself speaking through Albert?

Sixteen years later, the world understood the significance of the revelation from the fire beside the lake. Einstein was awarded the Nobel Prize. The year, 1905, became known as *annus mirabilis*, year of miracles.

In a sense the fire beside the Swiss lake gave us, arguably so, the most important story of our time: the creation story of the Big Bang with its dramatic flaring forth of fireball energy. Throughout his life Albert returned again and again to fire and water for inspiration.

When he moved to Princeton, New Jersey, he immediately sought the solace and inspiration of a nearby lake as he rowed his little boat day after day.

Would it be too much of a reach to assert that the theory of relativity was a joint effort of fire and water? Is this the Scripture of Nature coming through the Sacred Council?

In Einstein's discoveries the scientific revelation unveils key elements of Nature Herself. So great was the love that burned in the Fire that it leaped across to the modern human mind, allowing us to see deeply (but not completely) into the Mystery. The newer sciences provide us with a context for intimacy with Nature never before possible with humans.

27

A Story of Resilient Councils

Jeff is both Chief of Police and City Manager in the small town of Martindale, Texas. This story could be about him and his City Council and their struggle to move through a debt of $400,000 and not be gobbled up by a larger city.

Dan and Shiila own a small business barely keeping its head above water in era of The Great Recession and an era of bail outs. No bailouts seem to trickle down to small businesses on Main Street. This story could be about this capitalistic drama.

Tina and Doug live on a hilltop overlooking Lake Buchanan about one and a half hours northwest of Austin. They sailed for fourteen years in the Caribbean early in their relationship, and stories roll off their lips like honey on morning toast. But their sailing story is not the subject of this narrative.

No, this story is about a journey of talented but inexperienced amateurs in the use of survival skills for navigating the white waters of the emergent world. It is a story in the genre of Jimmy Breslin's *The Gang That Couldn't Shoot Straight*.

All of us—these five and many others—have known each other for years in a variety of vibrant communities rooted in the Earthtribe. Criteria for membership in the Earthtribe is love of the Earth. If you love the Earth, you are in. This story is about taking our community worldview and practices to a new level. We stand around a ceremonial fire one winter day discussing our options. Our *gang* spends a lot of time standing around campfires gazing into the coals and talking. We generate many arrows for aiming at Earth solutions but only a few hit the target. Unlike Einstein the fire does not bestow on us a Nobel Prize, far from it.

What can and will we—all of us in the Earth—do to face the critical conditions of Earth as they become more and more challenging? Is the fire once again at work in its inspiration? How deep will the crisis move? Are we near the bottom, or will the United States and the rest of the planet continue its downward spiral? Is the oil slick in the Gulf just the warning shot across our bow? Or is it a death blow to the gut of the world's fishery?

We discuss the possible levels of the planetary transition. Perhaps, we are bouncing off the bottom now, we assert to each other hopefully as the fire continues to warm us. On the other hand, maybe not. A worst case scenario brings into play a collapse of order as we know it in our current culture. What if the monetary system fails? As we talk around the fire, the Euro Zone teeters at the abyss. What if the infrastructure of water, power, and food that we take for granted loses much, even most, of its ability to support our lives.

This dialogue is not new to our little group. We have explored the emerging life conditions and their challenges in some detail for a few years. Sometimes, we are downright paranoid while at other moments, visionary. We are aware that apocalyptic communities predicting the end of the world have been around forever. It hasn't happened yet. Such a knowing is comforting. Today, we move into hopeful possibilities arising in our community through our collaborations.

Already our sustainability solutions group has installed rain water collection systems in all our households. Two households represented in the discussion are completely self-supporting in their water usage. Another is close, and a third has working plans to extend the rainwater collection from the garden to the household. Taken together our sustainability group stores nearly 50,000 gallons of water. We also are offering free water seminars for our area. We aren't largely influential, but we have assisted about ten households in the installation of their rain harvesting systems, mainly through sharing our plentiful mistakes.

Given a partial collapse, or even the *full monty*, we have water to drink and share. We started on this water journey knowing nothing about rainwater collection. We made mistakes. We lost thousands of gallons through a variety of snafus like faulty plumbing. A communal and practical wisdom with water collection resulted in a set of skills we can bring to the table in a monetary collapse.

In a visit to the Andes, Judith and I learned from the indigenous Quechua the practice of *ayni*, or reciprocity. We are prepared; we know about water collection. Our neighbors throughout the Blanco River valley where we live possess other resources. We can trade with them if the monetary systems break down. If not, we reciprocate for the simple joy of the intimacy involved and doing the right thing for Mother Earth. Our first aspiration is for the good of the environment. A corollary of that premise is our survival, along with deeper bonding in our community. We value the human species and aspire to conserve the best we humans have to offer the rest of the planet. Hanging out in a circle reflecting on the larger story ferments solutions to make us better humans.

We notice these sustainability initiatives strengthen our ties to each other and, in some mysterious dynamic, moves us toward a deeper intimacy. Something about working with our hands with rainwater, solar collection, and gardening evokes the joy of basic human survival. We are white collared professionals discovering the pleasure of blue collars. In our practical work we retrieve a bit of the primordial mind. Ancestors seem to stand with us as we shuffle our feet, laugh, and clap our hands over the fire for warmth.

Speaking of the international monetary boondoggle, the subject of investment safety arises as we add logs to the fire. One economist and mathematician, Charles Eisenstein, explores where to invest our money in the current situation, not to mention the challenge if the economic weather worsens into a full blown storm.

He has little confidence in the stock market and real estate. Corporate bonds are out in a crunch. Even U.S. Treasury notes look fragile with a national debt reaching 13 trillion dollars. Gold and silver present storage problems. As this economist ticked off the economic options not offering any security in the current world, we wonder if there are any investment opportunities to protect our vulnerabilities in stormy times. Does he have any answers?

What he suggests startles us.

The best investment, argues Eisenstein, in these perilous times is building resilient communities. By resilient community he means the very kind of support in water collection we are giving to each other. A secure investment is ayni, or the community barn raising spirit of the American frontier. As he puts it, "Security comes from the web of gifts, from being connected to others in your community. It's really simple, actually. If you have friends, they will help."[1]

Yet, such a process is not as simple as it sounds at first-glance. Building a network of friends with that dimension of awareness and practice is not easy—possible, but challenging. We have water, but what about electric power? Even more complicated is this question—What kind of intimate environment is needed for strategic navigation in times of massive trouble? We don't know, but we plunge forward.

The Earthtribe network has broadened to include input from Wisdom University, the Toltec Community, Jean Houston's Social Artistry, the work of Angeles Arrien, and others. I call it the *new ecumenism*. Our informal discussions include neural cells stretching from our brains to our hearts. At one point one in our midst suggests applying our emerging barn raising mentality to alternative energy.

After initial research Doug, Tina, and I install a beginning solar system in our house. Doug is a brilliant engineer, and Tina, a CPA, a master of details. I am good at talking with them about global issues as they work. The fledgling system is powerful enough to run a shop and small seminar setting. We invite a recent graduate in engineering from the University of Texas to drive out to the property to evaluate the solar system. He pronounces it sufficient to recharge an electric-plug-in auto as soon as the beleaguered automobile industry produces an affordable product.

Next, our sustainability group hatches a plan to design solar and wind systems we could build by going first to one house and then another with the aspiration of providing enough power for all of the electronic devices in our homes. In case the infrastructure deteriorates, we could have enough power to run our computers, our cell phones, and minimal heat. We could have enough electricity to heat up a small stove.

The SG's (Sustainability Group) play with the notion that the line between saving civilization or not lies in whether the internet continues. The internet has become the hardwire of our planetary brain connecting us with the rest of the world. The internet would be necessary for communal ties around the planet. My guess? If we have electric power, the internet will survive nearly any disaster. Pockets of small circles around the planet—such as the ones I describe here—would be up and running thanks to an integration of internet technology and investment in local, resilient community. Could such investments be the basis of a new, evolutionary stock market?

Spring weather awakens the subject of gardens. All of the SG'S have gardens of a sort. The problem is none of us really know what we are doing. One year we grew enough squash to feed a small army, and another we had broccoli coming out of our ears. Clearly, we need more knowledge and experience of planting cycles, soil, beneficial insects, and so-called pests.

But our sustainability gang that can't quite shoot straight is on its way. We are having fun, building strong ties that unite, and, on occasion, knowing each other at a deeper level. We are learning to trust each other in a variety of personal crises—illness, accidents, bankruptcy, depression, family squabbles, anxiety, and other garden variety human foibles. We are developing beginning skills in conflict resolution. We still don't shoot too straight with solar power and gardening, but we hit the mark with water. We have several households completely off the grid in terms of water. We call ourselves the clean hair cadre because rainwater is heavenly for showers and shampoos.

In one conversation we decide to take our vision of meeting basic needs to the larger community, even to you. We aspire to invest our money, time, and energy in the evolutionary stock market of resilient community. We invite you to join us in building intimate communities.

Cultural creatives, unite!

We want to link with you in an aware and awake way.

We want to be a secure raft in the storm.

Many of you are building resilient communities. The storm is wild, but we have Wild Hearts. In our Wild Hearts we can find primordial resources. We join you in retrieving the uncontrollable, the untamed. We feel the wind on our faces. The rain beats against our matted hair and sunburned skin. We are not melting even if the sweat leaves salt in our eyes. We blink but keep looking. We balance ourselves with the amazing aware-go who makes room for the wisdom of civilized voices as well as wild ones. We can see you out there. Together we become stronger, wiser, and join the next great migration up the Sacred Spiral of the human journey.

EPILOGUE: The Sacred Spiral

The Great Mother of Memory calls forth into awareness the profound truth of the expanding quality of the Universe. The Universe expands and evolves in two ways I know of: *complexity* and *awareness*. This profound expansion moves up and down the spiral of evolution, providing us with resources for the challenge of our current life conditions amply described in previous chapters.

As we descend the spiral to a more basic era sometimes called The Primordial Mind, we can retrieve the Wild Heart (the heartbeat of the Primordial Mind) sub-self so essential to this moment in the human story. Don Beck, evolutionary scientist, has translated the research of Clare W. Graves into a concise map of the spiral of cultural evolution, noting a color for each turn of the spiral.[1] The stories you just read follow each orbit on the spiral, starting with primal humans. In the next book of this series, I will explore in greater detail the stages of development in the 200,000 year human story.

Following is a brief introduction to the use of this spiral map for our discussion of the Wild Heart Stories of Hope.

- Beige- The first 150,000 years of the human story focused on survival as humans learned to eat and be eaten with all the relatives of their ecology. A central discovery was the respectful circle of life. The story of the farmer's market in Oakland looks at reconnecting with the highest values of this era: learning to respect that which we need to kill in order to survive. Descending to this era is necessary for survival in the turbulence of our day.

- Purple- The next 50,000 years saw humans discover the magic of interconnectivity with beginning self-reflection in rock art. The guidance of shamanic allies within the non-human world showed the way. Interspecies communication was the norm. The story of the hummingbird and the policewoman directs our attention to that resource for our current journey. Recent archeological discoveries in Turkey reveal this shamanic era (The Primordial Mind/Heart) of profound spirituality as being the Mother of Civilization.[2] I am not suggesting we return culture to this era but rather we retrieve the power of being a specie among species, an animal among animals. This shamanic era mothered altered states of consciousness, the wild fuel of the dream and vision world so necessary to move us in our current crisis.

- Red/Blue- With the discovery of agriculture (Circa 7,000 BCE) humans developed a warrior and mythic view of the world. A crucial value of this era was the domesticating of animals. The story of the gift of the buffalo probes the terrain between the domains of the wild and the domesticated. It raises the question of how we can develop a love of both the wild and the domestic, an integral love between the species. It calls us to be hybrids of the wild and the civilized.

- Orange/Green- With the advent of the modern era (begins in 1859 with the first oil in Pennsylvania) the value of the rational, scientific, and objective view of the world blossomed from seeds reaching back to the golden age of Greece. The story of Einstein's relationship with friends, mountain lakes, and campfires probes the modern and post-modern cultural gift of the scientific revelation, but goes a step beyond the usual scientific approach. My viewfinder—shaped by integrating the shamanic and scientific—opens a new possibility between humans, fire, and water. These elements are crucial in the current environmental crisis. The archeological finds in Turkey strongly suggest a Primordial Pool of Consciousness as spawning civilization, including the revelations of modern science. A close reading of the Einstein story confirms that notion.

- 2nd Tier (Yellow/Turquoise)- Clare W Graves and his student, Don Beck, point to a quantum leap in cultural evolution to an orbit now in its infant stages.[3] Some call this, *The Integral Age*; others, *The Age of the Emerging Wisdom Culture*; others, *The EcoZoic Era*.

A term I sometimes use to describe this aspect of the human journey is ***The Eco-Evolutionary Community, a global learning community***. I like this description because it emphasizes the emergent qualities described in the last story. The conversations and practices called forth by the wild of the fire pull us energetically to the beige, then to purple, then to orange and green. We now are poised to make a quantum leapt to the 2nd Tier, a domain of evolution Beck calls Yellow/Turquoise. We integrate the inspiration of the deep relationships spawned through interspecies communication with the newest science involved in solar energy, to site one example. In this way we learn how to move up and down the spiral of evolution, knowing each level of the human story has its gifts, skills, and brilliance.

This movement of ascending and descending the spiral of cultural evolution allows humans and non-humans alike to integrate values at each level. When we fully integrate the Wild Heart from our early life on the planet, the possibility of an eco-evolutionary human emerges with a vision in hand of Nature as a matrix of loving relatives and resilient communities.

Mitakuye Oyasin, All Are My Relations.
Puha, The Sacred Wind breathes power and love through us.

Notes

Introduction to the Book Series: The Sacred Mentor
   1. Swimme, Brian. Canticle To The Cosmos, #6,
     San Francisco: New Story, 1990.

Part I   The Call of the Era of Crisis

Chapter 1   Sounding the Conch
   1. National Geographic

Chapter 3   The Proposal
   1. Weil, Andrew, M.D., Why We Are All Addicted
     www.online.sfsu.edu/~rone/Buddhism/FivePrecepts/
     addicted.html

   2. Dubois, Rene, So Human An Animal
     (New York: Transaction Publishers, 1998), pp. 2-47.

Chapter 4   The Awakening
   1. www.archaeology.about.com/od/ancientdailylife/qt/
     fire_control.htm

   2. www.atmo.tamu.edu

Part II   The Sacred Council Gathers

Chapter 5   Roots of the Sacred Council
   1. www.iroquois-confederacy.html
   2. www.iroquois-confederacy.html
   3. www.ratical.org/many_worlds/6Nations/

Chapter 6   The Inner Council of Selves
   1. Plato, The Repubic. New York: Cambridge University Press,
     2006, Book 2, pp. 37-47.

Chapter 9   The Nature-based Selves: Wild Heart
1. Wilson, E. O., The Future of Life. New York: Knopf, 2002, p. 214.

Chapter 11   Opposites in the Sacred Council
1. Abernathy, Ralph, And the Walls Came Tumbling Down www.snopes.com/history/american/mlking.asp

Chapter 12   The Amazing Aware-go
1. Whitehead, Alfred North, Process and Reality. New York: Free Press, p. 32-47.
2. Ray, Paul. Faculty Conversation, Oakland, Ca.,May 2009.
3. Wilber, Ken, Grace and Grit. Boston: Shambhala,1993, p. 405.
4. Wilber, Ken, Grace and Grit, p. 405.
5. Wilber, Ken. Integral Spirituality, Boston: Integral Books, 2006, Ch. 4.
6. Burns, Ken . National Parks: America's Best Idea. PBS, Blue Ray DVD.

Chapter 13   The Sacred Council In Action
1. Quoted by Martin Luther King, Jr. Autobiography of Martin Luther King, Jr. New York: Warner Press, 1998, Chapter 2.
2. "Gandhi", International Wildlife, May-June, 1997.
3. Kennedy, President John F., State of the Union Address, Jan. 11, 1962.

Chapter 14   Tails in the Avatar Tale
1. Bateson, Gregory, Mind and Nature:A Necessary Unity. New York: Dutton Press, 1979, cover.
2. Bohm, David, Infinite Potential. Reading, Mass.: Helix Books,1997, p.10.
3. Gebser, Jean, The Ever Present Origi.Columbus, Ohio: Swallow Press, 1986, p. 107.
4. Lucas, George. NPR, Jan. 6, 2010.
5. Gebser, Jean, The Ever Present Origin, p. 48.

Part III Sacred Councils Bond

Chapter 15   Councils in Conflict
  1. www.greenspirit.com
  2. Buffett, Warren,
     www.cnn.com/2005/US/05/10/buffett/index.html
  3. Stone, Hal and Sidra, Personal Conversations.

Chapter 16   Fire in the Council
  1. Crichton, Michael, State of Fear, New York: Harper Collins,
     2004, Introduction.
  2. www.jameslovelock.org

Chapter 18   Negative Bonding Patterns Between Councils
  1. Santa Fe Lectures, Wisdom University, January, 2010.
  2. www.law.umkc.edu/faculty/projects/ftrials/socrates/
     socratesaccount.html

Chapter 19   Hidden Selves As Fuel in the Council
  1. Austin American Statesman, 4-13-10, p. A7.
  2. Stone, I. F., The Trial of Socrates, New York: New York
     Times Press, 1980.
  3. www.law.umkc.edu/faculty/projects/ftrials/socrates/
     socratesaccount.html
  4. Mc,Phee, John, The Control of Nature, New York:Giroux
     Paperbacks, 1990.

Chapter 20   Enamoured Councils: Positive Bonding Paterns
  1. Stone, Hal and Sidra, Lectures at the American
     Academy of Psychotherapists, Philadelphia, 1987.

Chapter 21   The Intimate Council
  1. Swimme, Brian, Canticle to the Cosmos, #1.
  2. www.sciencedaily.com/releases/2010/03/100325091430.htm
  3. www.seanparnell.com
  4. Swimme, Brian, Canticle to the Cosmos, #10
  5. Wilson, E. O., The Future of Life, p. 214.

6. Bear Heart with Larkin, Mary, The Wind Is My Mother
New York: Berkely Books,1996.

Part IV The Web of Sacred Councils: Wild Heart Stories of Hope In Crisis

Chapter 24   A Story of Allies in the Council

1. Plato, The Republic, (book 02).

Chapter 26   A Story of The Council of Fire and Water

1. Arrien, Angeles, Lectures at Wisdom University, July, 2009.

Chapter 27   A Story of Co-operative Councils

1. Ode, January/February, 2010, p.37.

Epilogue: The Sacred Spiral

1. Beck, Don & Christopher Cowan, Spiral Dynamics:
Mastering Values, Leadership, and Change, Malden, Mass.:
Blackwell Publishers, 1996, Section 1.

2. www.smithsonianmag.com/history-archaeology/
gobekli-tepe.html

3. Beck, Don Edward and Christopher C. Cowan,
Spiral Dynamics, chapters 15 &16.

5280475R0

Made in the USA
Charleston, SC
23 May 2010